BEING A
TEACHER

Sara Miller McCune founded SAGE Publishing in 1965 to support the dissemination of usable knowledge and educate a global community. SAGE publishes more than 1000 journals and over 800 new books each year, spanning a wide range of subject areas. Our growing selection of library products includes archives, data, case studies and video. SAGE remains majority owned by our founder and after her lifetime will become owned by a charitable trust that secures the company's continued independence.

Los Angeles | London | New Delhi | Singapore | Washington DC | Melbourne

CAROL THOMPSON & PETER WOLSTENCROFT

BEING A
TEACHER

the trainee teacher's guide to developing the personal and professional skills you need

Learning Matters

Learning Matters
A SAGE Publishing Company
1 Oliver's Yard
55 City Road
London EC1Y 1SP

SAGE Publications Inc.
2455 Teller Road
Thousand Oaks,
California 91320

SAGE Publications India Pvt Ltd
B 1/I 1 Mohan Cooperative Industrial Area
Mathura Road
New Delhi 110 044

SAGE Asia-Pacific Pte Ltd
3 Church Street
#10–04 Samsung Hub
Singapore 049483

Editor: Amy Thornton
Senior project editor: Chris Marke
Project management: River Editorial
Marketing manager: Lorna Patkai
Cover design: Wendy Scott
Typeset by: C&M Digitals (P) Ltd, Chennai, India
Printed in the UK

Library of Congress Control Number: TBC

British Library Cataloguing in Publication Data

A catalogue record for this book is available from the British Library

ISBN 978-1-5297-5197-0
ISBN 978-1-5297-5198-7 (pbk)

At SAGE we take sustainability seriously. Most of our products are printed in the UK using responsibly sourced papers and boards. When we print overseas we ensure sustainable papers are used as measured by the PREPS grading system. We undertake an annual audit to monitor our sustainability.

CONTENTS

ABOUT THE AUTHORS

Carol Thompson is a Senior Lecturer in Teacher Education at the University of Bedfordshire. An experienced teacher and researcher, she has a focus on developing teacher agency and creativity. Her current role is focused on designing and supporting programmes for teachers in post-compulsory education and she is an active member of the Institute of Research in Education.

Peter Wolstencroft is an Associate Professor at Liverpool John Moores University. A firm believer in the transformative power of education, his recent work has looked to encourage innovation education. An active researcher and blogger, he has written on topics as diverse as digital literacy and educational leadership, the common thread in all his work being that education can transform lives.

INTRODUCTION

Teaching can sometimes be viewed as a controversial occupation and it is one that is open to much judgement from others. Perhaps rightly so – after all, it is a very important undertaking. Teachers have such an active role in the shaping of young minds, in enhancing the skills of society and supporting the development of the country's workforce. They form the scaffold of every education system and sometimes help to cushion the blows inflicted by a complex and confused world. Teachers can play a significant part in liberating or constraining thought and in doing so can enhance or limit freedom. But what does it really mean to be a teacher?

A teacher's life is complex and it cannot easily be contained within a few prescriptive statements – yet it so often is. Most teachers are trained against a set of professional standards and once qualified are judged according to internal and external policies. This is not unusual in any professional field, but when the role has a focus on human relationships there are other factors to be taken into account. Teacher expertise should embrace the profession as a whole and this encompasses a combination of skills including those not directly linked to classroom practice. Too often, the focus is placed very firmly on the development of *teaching* competences – those things which have a direct impact on the act of teaching, rather than *teacher* competences – the things which frame what it means to be a teacher. There is some sense in this; enhancing classroom practice is essential if you are to develop confidence but by making this a focus, we neglect some very important things not only for teachers but for the profession as a whole. In our view it is just as important, perhaps even more important, to build *teacher* competences, those things which encompass what it really means to be a teacher. These are represented by the knowledge and skills taken beyond the classroom door, the things which influence how we view and carry out our work.

Enhancing teacher competence involves developing an understanding of the education landscape and how this influences local practice. In addition, it requires teachers to establish strong values in relation to their roles and to link these to a secure professional identity. To make all of this happen, teachers need to claim their agency, to take charge of their practice and to continually focus on their professional development. It is unlikely that any course of teacher education, however good it is, will be able to equip teachers with all the skills they will need and even if it could, the world of education continues to evolve and so too must teachers.

In order to fully understand what it means to be a teacher, it is necessary to critically reflect on, and challenge assumptions about your own practice as well as the profession as a whole. This will help to widen perspectives and provide alternative approaches and is an essential part of professionalism. Open and honest reflection can be quite a challenge but we hope that the ideas within this book provide some useful guidance to support this process.

In *Being a Teacher* we explore key aspects of the teacher's role from a range of perspectives and aim to extend current thinking by borrowing ideas from other disciplines. Taking inspiration from Koestler's classic work, *The Act of Creation* (1964), we are structuring the book around the notion of bisociation – the combination of an object or idea from two fields not always considered to be related. To do this we have drawn on psychology, philosophy, business and even literature to inform the writing.

Each chapter acknowledges aspects of current practice and introduces new ideas to consider. These are illustrated through the use of case studies and reflective activities to allow you to personalise the information to your own context. In addition, there are some suggested approaches you could try out for yourself. We hope that this makes the material both accessible and thought provoking.

Being a teacher is more than meeting the Teachers' Standards; more than demonstrating good class-room practice; and more than getting learners to pass assessments. Great teachers have faith in learning and its endless potential. It is a profession grounded in hope and in the belief that change for the better is always possible.

1

THINKING ABOUT TEACHING

In this chapter we will explore:

- Perceptions of the purpose of education
- How this impacts on classroom practice
- Ways of responding positively to change

INTRODUCTION

You may have already completed your initial teacher training or be close to doing so and you probably have a good idea about what the role involves – you may be in your first year – or perhaps you are a more experienced teacher who is mentoring a trainee? Whichever it is, you are likely to have already formed an opinion on the key components of the teaching role and how to manage it most effectively, but how often are you able to stop and think what it *really* means to be a teacher? It is quite likely that your view on the role has been influenced by things such as the environment you work in, your phase of education (early years, primary, secondary or post-compulsory), your initial teacher training, the Teacher Standards (or the Professional Standards) and your experiences on placement or in the job. Hopefully, amongst all of that, you have maintained some of your initial ideas about teaching and have remembered the reasons why you thought this would be a great job for you. In this chapter we will explore some of the things that have influenced education as a whole and the impact that has had on the teacher's role. We will also consider how you can maintain autonomy and authenticity in the role and continue to take a creative approach to it.

A LiTTLE BiT OF HiSTORY

Whilst it isn't the aim of this book to go into great depth on historical developments in education, it is useful to have an understanding of how things have evolved over the years and the impact this has had on the role of the teacher. The examples provided in this section are mostly based on the English education system but there are a number of similarities with education in other countries. In our experience of working with colleagues in Europe and North America, the process has been quite similar, even if the specific steps are different.

Historically, the teacher's role would have been depicted as a purveyor of knowledge, enforcer of rules, maybe even a disciplinarian. More recently, ideas about the facilitation of learning have become more popular alongside a focus on either a customer or consumer model whereby teachers 'deliver' knowledge linked to specific outcomes, which in turn leads to the achievement of a range of qualifications. This is a challenging shift as 'learning' is very difficult to package as a tangible product; you can't simply pick it off a shelf and pay the appropriate price, yet the overall commercialisation of education does suggest that in some ways education is viewed as a product, or at the very least, a service that learners buy into. The difficulty here is that this service cannot be one-way, teachers cannot simply provide learning; the process requires a two-way interaction for it to be effective. The teacher may be required to 'deliver' but the student must contribute as well – an important point to remember when faced with classes who simply want to receive information passively and are reluctant to interact!

Education has evolved over time and Figure 1.1 provides an outline of some of the key influences over the last 100 years or so.

THE PURPOSE OF EDUCATION

We can see some of the key changes to education policy in Figure 1.1 and it is worth thinking about what these say about the overall purpose of education. When we are caught up in the day to day activities of teaching, this is often something that is forgotten. The many tasks teachers have to complete don't always seem to have an obvious connection to teaching and learning and it can be very easy to forget how what we do connects to the bigger picture.

REFLECTION

Try to forget most of the day to day tasks that take up your job role and get right back to basics. What do you see as the main purpose of education?

There are varying views on the purpose of education. To some it is seen as an end in itself, something to be cherished and nurtured on a lifelong basis. Others view education as a means to an end, perhaps the completion of an examination or the gaining of skills that will enhance career opportunities. Perhaps it is even reasonable to suggest that education is both of these things ... and more. That said, day to day teaching can feel like a whirlwind of activity with an ever-increasing list of tasks to complete and, at times, it might even seem that the purpose of education is to gather lots of data and complete even more paperwork!

A brief history of education

1780 THE FIRST SUNDAY SCHOOL
The early pioneers of education, Robert Raikes, Thomas Stock and others, set up the original Sunday Schools to bring education to people who otherwise would not have been educated.

1820s MECHANICS INSTITUTES FOUNDED
George Birkbeck founded the first Mechanics Institute and the subsequent years saw an increase in the number of educational establishments.

1902 EDUCATION ACT (THE BALFOUR ACT)
This established Local Education Authorities (LEAs) who could raise taxes in order to fund schools. This was the beginning of moving funding away from the church.

1944 EDUCATION ACT (THE BUTLER ACT)
Created separate primary and secondary schools and LEAs had to ensure nursery provision. The school leaving age was raised to 15.

1967 THE PLOWDEN REPORT
An advisory report into primary education and the transition to secondary education.

1976 THE RUSKIN SPEECH
Then Prime Minister James Callaghan's speech at Ruskin College called for a great debate about the purpose of education and how it should link to the needs of society.

1988 THE EDUCATION REFORM ACT (BAKER ACT)
Introduction of Grant Maintained schools, local control and Key stages.

1992 EDUCATION (SCHOOLS) ACT
This established Ofsted (the Office for Standards in Education) to ensure compliance by inspecting schools on a regular cycle. It would publish its reports and had the power to name and shame underperforming schools.

1992 THE FURTHER AND HIGHER EDUCATION ACT
Made changes to funding and administration. A number of polytechnics became universities. In the following year the incorporation of colleges allowed them to become independent of LEAs and created a more competitive environment.

2011 THE ACADEMIES ACT
This Act changed the structures of many schools. They remained publicly funded but with a vastly increased degree of autonomy in issues such as setting teachers' wages and diverging from the National Curriculum.

2020 PANDEMIC
The 2020 pandemic completely changed how education was viewed and structured, with an increased focus on remote learning and the use of digital technology.

Figure 1.1   A brief history of education

EDUCATION AS A ROUTE TO MERITOCRACY

Early pioneers such as Robert Raikes, Hannah More and George Birkbeck stressed the importance of educating the workforce to ensure that a degree of meritocracy could be introduced into British society (this is where the most able members of society are chosen to lead rather than selection being based on historical factors such as social class), but they also talked about the increased role individuals could take on when educated. Remember that during the Industrial Revolution, universal education was not always seen as a good thing as there was a worry that if you educate the masses then they might begin to get ideas 'above their station'. In this sense education is seen as something of a leveller – the idea being that by educating everyone we are providing a more level playing field and individuals can progress based on their ability rather than their position in society. This is of course assuming that education is the only factor at play here – it doesn't take into account culture, access to resources, class prejudice and so on.

EDUCATION AS A VEHICLE FOR SOCIAL CHANGE

The notion that education can be used as a vehicle for social change is one that came out of the campaigns from the early pioneers. Mary Wollstonecraft stressed education's role in her fight for greater rights for women, whilst in South Wales the importance of education in helping the working classes gain influence in UK society is encapsulated in the inscription over the old library in Pillgwenlly, Newport: 'Libraries give us power'. These are indeed commendable aims and it is interesting to consider whether education is seen in the same way today. Think about your role as a teacher: have you got the power to help your students to achieve their life goals, or maybe a better question is, are you able to change your students' life goals by showing them alternative ways of thinking and being?

EDUCATION FOR ECONOMIC DEVELOPMENT

If you take another look into the motives of the forerunners of education change, you might begin to see that providing education was rarely a philanthropic action but had a more fundamental purpose. For Birkbeck it was encouraging his workers to know more about the machinery they were being asked to use. Other pioneers stressed differing objectives; William Hesketh Lever, who built much of Port Sunlight to house and educate his workforce, used education as a way of encouraging people to take an interest in the business as well as the wider world. In that way he encouraged greater worker participation and what he termed 'prosperity sharing'. Whilst Lever's philanthropic aims are clear to see, the underlying desire for a more organised, more highly skilled workforce clearly shows philanthropy grounded in pragmatism.

EDUCATION FOR SOCIAL CONTROL

For Raikes and More, there was a strong religious element to education, with a focus on being able to read and understand the Bible. At first glance this might seem like an outrageous suggestion – after all, education is about freeing minds not controlling them. However, the idea isn't that unusual or that new. Notions of power are embedded into our culture and for some, formal education is the ideal arena for reinforcing this. In *The Republic*, Plato portrayed his ideas about the ideal society in which a 'guardian' class would organise matters of importance whereas others, such as artisans and workers, would be educated to know their place within society.

REFLECTION

All of this raises a number of questions:

- Are we educating people to have the skills required to enhance economic development?
- Is education a form of social and moral control?
- Is education the basis for encouraging change within society?
- Or is it for the benefit of individuals with a focus on engendering a love of learning that will last for the rest of their lives?

It is not our intention to tell you the answers to these questions; however, it is something that you might like to think about as it will help you understand your motives for becoming a teacher. What is even more important is recognising the impact of what you do in the classroom.

THE GREAT DEBATE

One significant development in the way our education system has developed is captured in what is referred to as 'the great debate' that followed the then Prime Minister, James Callaghan's speech at Ruskin College in 1976. Callaghan talked about how education can be used as a vehicle to support industry and how part of the government's role should be to encourage this objective. His speech has been cited by numerous subsequent governments as an inspiration for policy initiatives that have sought to exert influence over aspects such as the content of the curriculum, the way education is managed and funded and the ways that teachers are trained. Examples of this include the introduction of a National Curriculum in the Education Reform Act (1988), the introduction of increased influence from the private sector in the Further and Higher Education Act (1992) and the current discussions regarding the funding of degrees, which have stressed the importance of starting salaries as a measure for judging the success of higher education courses.

THE BIGGER PICTURE

We all have our individual views on the purpose of education and as a part of this it is important to recognise the connections it has to other aspects of life. Its purpose is widespread and incorporates:

- Economics – education provides individuals with skills to earn a living and provides the economy with a more skilled workforce.
- Culture – education develops our understanding of the world around us.
- Personal development – education develops individual talents and abilities (Robinson 2017).

What is clear is that at different points in time, these elements become more or less significant as they mirror what is happening in society. When economic development is a focus, then so too are workplace skills; when social issues rise, so does the need to enhance cultural knowledge and acceptance of diversity. After all, education is the panacea to the world's ills!

Whilst some views of our current systems of education can seem a little negative, there are very few people who would question its value and the importance it plays in meeting the needs of society. As Robinson suggests: 'In the twenty-first century, humanity faces some of its most daunting challenges. Our best resource is to cultivate our singular abilities of imagination, creativity and innovation .... Education is the key to the future, the stakes could hardly be higher' (Robinson, 2017: 38).

In a similar vein it is also difficult for most people to differentiate education from teachers and to accredit the success of the former with the skills of the latter.

Figure 1.2 Tangled web

What does this mean for teachers today? The honest answer is that it can mean different things to different people. There are many stakeholders in education (including, but not limited to, students, parents, politicians and employers) all with varied wants and needs and then there are the education leaders and teachers who try to make it all happen. This in itself creates something of a tangled web. We also need to consider that we operate in a changeable environment where the focus fluctuates with the wind – this makes it difficult to pinpoint exactly what we *should* be doing at any one time and it's hard to keep track of whether this week's focus is about developing literacy and numeracy skills or health and well-being ... and of course, getting caught up in that debate probably isn't going to be helpful in finding a way through the maze. What does seem to be apparent is that all of the change is based on a dual premise:

- Education is a good thing and has a widespread influence.

- To improve the quality of education we need to improve the quality of teaching.

Whilst the second point might seem harsh, most of the teachers we have worked with would probably agree with it and most of them strive to be the best teachers that they can be. They do this despite initiative overload and constant change – they do it because professionalism is a core value and they genuinely believe and hope that they can influence in positive ways. As bell hooks states: 'Educating is always a vocation rooted in hopefulness. As teachers we believe that learning is possible, that nothing can keep an open mind from seeking after knowledge and finding a way to know' (hooks, 2003: xiv).

THE iMPACT ON TEACHERS' ROLES

At first glance these discussions might seem to have only a tenuous connection to your classroom, but when you consider some of the motives behind educational movements the connections become apparent. If we treat education as a means to an end, then we need to think about how that might influence the overall process? Are there likely to be more controls of what is taught and even how it is taught? Is there likely to be more of a focus on assessment? This will also have an impact on teachers' roles in terms of how much autonomy they have, both in planning and organising learning. How we are encouraged to view learners is also an important consideration – if a business model is taken, then learners become customers (or maybe consumers), if a more social model is adopted then the focus is on the development of individuals for the good of society as a whole. All of this impacts on classroom activity – a business model is more likely to have a product focus in that it will be driven by the achievement of measurable outcomes such as qualifications. If we adopt more of a social model with outcomes that are less easy to measure, the focus is more likely to be centred on the process of learning with learning itself being the goal.

TEACHER-PROOFiNG

'The quality of an education system cannot exceed the quality of its teachers' (Barber and Mourshed, 2007: 16). This message seems to be something that many of the influencers in education have listened to. The huge raft of initiatives and 'evidence-based' practice that has dominated the last 20 years or more may be evidence of this. The process of 'teacher-proofing' (Bennett, 2013) has involved the application of 'educational pseudo-science' to teaching practice, whereby 'Values become facts, which are then taught and propagated in educational training establishments …. and hoisted on the unsuspecting profession, who have little leverage to say no' (Ibid.: 2).

It is difficult to disagree with Bennett's view here but, for us, that disagreement is probably linked to the second part of the quote. Research informed practice need not be a bad thing and some research has most certainly had a positive impact, indeed some strategies which may fall in Bennett's category of 'educational pseudo-science' have worked well for us and for many of our students. The problem arises when choice is removed, when teachers are told to do things in very specific ways, following even more specific formulae and when the need to think for themselves and bring their own creativity to a lesson is much diminished.

Figure 1.3 Crushing creativity

ACTIVITY

Here are three evidence-based approaches to teaching. Which means that they are all based on research in some shape or form. Take a look at the description of the research and consider how this might be used in your practice. Then consider two questions:

What are the positives of this approach?

What are the drawbacks?

Metacognition (Marzano, 1998) – The most basic component of metacognition is awareness of thinking processes. It has been referred to as 'thinking about thinking'. In theory, effective learners are aware of how they think and can make good choices about effective strategies for approaching their work. In practice this involves learners being aware of their thinking processes, planning how they will address tasks and monitoring how effective their chosen strategies were.

Cognitive Load Theory (Sweller, 1988) – Cognitive load theory is based on the idea that the brain can only do so many things at once, therefore over-complicated learning activities will be distracting, increase a learner's cognitive load and make it difficult for them to pay attention and remember the learning. This means that teachers need to be specific about what is being learned and about the sequence of learning. In practice this means managing the learning environment to reduce distractions. In addition learning will be supported by creating a bridge between prior learning and new learning, presenting information in chunks using graphic organisers and using examples to illustrate new learning.

Rosenshine Principles of Instruction (Rosenshine, 2010) – This focuses on ten key principles taken from cognitive science, observation of master teachers and studies that taught learning strategies. The ten principles are:

1. Begin a lesson with a short review of previous learning
2. Present new material in small steps with student practice after each step
3. Ask a large number of questions and check the responses of all students
4. Provide models
5. Guide student practice
6. Check for understanding
7. Obtain a high success rate
8. Provide scaffolds for difficult tasks
9. Require and monitor independent practice
10. Engage students in weekly and monthly review.

CASE STUDY

Karima is a newly qualified teacher (NQT) who always seems to be the first to arrive in the morning and the last to leave at night, often saying that she still has a lot of work to do when she gets home. She confides in her mentor that she is really struggling with planning her lessons and sometimes finds it impossible to cover everything. So much so, that she is beginning to wonder if teaching is for her. She doesn't know how she will teach all the topics she needs to teach as well as enhance learners' literacy and numeracy skills, help support their developing resilience, discuss

(Continued)

(Continued)

citizenship and consider well-being. Karima is also worried that her planning is not 'up to standard' as she doesn't always follow the lesson guidelines she was given when she first arrived.

Karima is evidence of the negative impact of 'teacher-proofing'. Whilst the introduction of guidelines and evidence-based teaching strategies are intended to support teaching and learning, they also have the potential to detract from it by overloading teachers with long lists of 'shoulds' and leaving very little wriggle room for more individual approaches.

All of the changes we have mentioned have had an impact on the day to day practice of teachers within schools, colleges and universities. In addition, the demands of wider society, such as the drive towards a more qualified workforce, have certainly acted as drivers, not only for education institutions, but also for the people working within them. After all, it is quite difficult to focus on your values towards teaching and learning when you are under constant pressure to produce specific results in very particular ways!

REFLECTION

Taking into account the historical changes outlined in this chapter and your personal experience of education (as a teacher or a student). What things have had the most influence on how you approach teaching now?

RESPONDING POSITIVELY TO CHANGE

As in much of life, in teaching there are some things you have no control over ... but the good news is there are lots of things you can do to maintain your initial values about teaching and learning and be the best teacher that you can be. Our belief is that if your focus is on doing your best then the end result will not only meet but probably exceed any targets you have been set. The trick is to consider the things you can change rather than getting lost in a world of 'shoulds' and to accept that this is a process.

YOUR VALUES ABOUT TEACHING AND LEARNING

A key part in developing your professional role is establishing clear values about teaching and learning. It can be easy to forget what's important when immersed in the day to day reality of teaching. One strategy that helps is to establish 'anchors' that inform your decision making. These are immoveable values that help you assess your response to anything proposed. Examples of these might be:

'The students always come first'

'Always treat people with respect'

'A love of learning promotes good learning'.

In the maelstrom of initiatives that invade education, clear anchors provide a focal point and will give you the confidence to choose your response to events instead of getting caught in a tidal wave.

—————— ACTiViTY ——————

Based on your experience to date what are your 'anchors'? Write them down and put them somewhere you can see. There will be times when you need to be reminded of these.

YOUR PROFESSiONAL iDENTiTY

The majority of the issues discussed in this chapter have originated from outside organisations rather than from teachers themselves and demonstrate that there are a number of things outside your control that will have a significant influence on your role. In all of this it is really important to develop and maintain a clear professional identity – by this we mean an understanding of your role as a teacher and the way that you identify with the profession as a whole. What is important to remember is that professional identity goes beyond your specific role within your current setting – it will not be removed if you move on. Professional identity is normally associated with values and things like professional ethics – in a way it is a professional reference point. A clear understanding of who you are as a teacher will mean that you maintain a consistency of approach and that you are able to manage whatever is thrown at you, thereby feeling in control of events rather than events controlling you. The anchors you outlined in the previous activity will certainly help with this.

Professional identity is also linked to your view of the profession as a whole and we are going to assume that this is a positive one and that such positivity is something you wish to maintain. To do this you really need to work hard at how you think about the role, which in turn will influence how you feel about it. There are some important steps you can take to keep your approach upbeat – some of these things will be explored in more detail in later chapters but for now, here are our top six strategies:

1. *See it as an adventure* – one of the great things about teaching is that you are always learning and what better adventure is there?

2. *Recognise that how you think influences how you feel* – a key premise of Cognitive Behavioural Therapy (CBT) is that the messages we give ourselves have a significant impact on our emotions, which in turn will influence our actions and further thoughts. According to Seligman: 'Habits of thinking need not be forever. One of the most significant findings in psychology in the last twenty years is that individuals can choose the way they think' (Seligman, 2018: 8).

3. *Develop your EQ* – your emotional quotient (EQ) is a measure of emotional intelligence which can be developed by raising self-awareness, managing negative emotions and practising empathy.

4. *Hone your critical thinking skills* – by analysing assumptions and viewing things from a range of perspectives.

5. *Be wary of 'shoulds'* – these are usually based on the requirements of others or misplaced beliefs.

6. *Feed your soul* – whilst your professional role is important, it isn't all you are. It is really important to feed your soul through whatever inspires you. Indulge in art, literature, film, theatre, nature.

CHAPTER SUMMARY

The focus of this chapter has been on the wide range of things which impact on the teaching role and our aim has been to encourage you to think about the role in a more general sense and its purpose in the overall framework of education. To keep this perspective in mind it is important to think about why we are teaching as much as we think about what and how we are teaching. Our suggestion to keep this focus in mind is to establish 'anchors' linked to your values about teaching and learning, as these will help guide you on your journey to becoming a teacher. To this end, we will leave you with three questions for reflection:

- Why did you become a teacher?

- How would you describe the teaching role?

- Have your views on the role changed over time? If so, what has influenced this change of view?

FURTHER READING

Bennett, T. (2013) *Teacher Proof: Why Research in Education Doesn't Always Mean What It Claims. And What You Can Do About It.* Oxon: Routledge.

Robinson, K. (2010) *Changing Paradigms.* (online) Available at: https://www.thersa.org/video/animates/2010/10/rsa-animate---changing-paradigms (accessed 14 October 2020).

2
THE MAP IS NOT THE TERRITORY

In this chapter we will explore:

- The influence of world views on teaching practice
- How an understanding of learning influences teaching
- Professional agency and its role in developing professional identity

INTRODUCTION

Figure 2.1   Map and territory

We see teaching as a creative role that evolves as your skills, expertise and confidence grow, and recognise that initial perceptions of the role change as a part of the process of *becoming* a teacher. For most teachers, there is teacher training and then there is teaching ... one leads to the other of course but becoming a teacher is something that happens in the NQT phase and beyond. In a previous book (Thompson and Wolstencroft, [2018] 2021) we introduced the phrase 'the map is not the territory' (Korzybski, 1931) and as you can see from the reference this isn't a new idea. The original use of the phrase was to show the relationship between an object and the representation of that object – a map is used to represent a geographical area but it isn't the actual landbase – it is simply a depiction of it. A similar phrase to explain this is 'the word is not the thing' – we use words all the time to describe things but they are not the objects themselves. Korzybski felt that people often confused representations of things with the things themselves. So, we might confuse maps with territories or our model of reality with reality itself. This is an interesting idea ... so let's explore how it applies to teaching.

The process of becoming a teacher is unlike any other and it can be quite difficult to understand what it is you need to know in order to make a success of the role. For this reason, it is essential that you are open to new ideas and that you learn how to develop your thinking in ways that encourage reflection, evaluation and openness. When you are training, it is important to know what your specific aims are and in this scenario some sort of 'map' is a very useful tool – take the Teachers' Standards or the Professional Standards as an example – these are useful guidelines for new and experienced teachers as they set out a framework of knowledge and skills that prepare you for the essential aspects of teaching. Without them, it might be difficult to know where to start ... but we also need to remind ourselves that such guides, whilst a good start, are not all there is. They are a map of sorts ... they are not the territory. The actual role of teaching is far more complex than that and the process of becoming a teacher is a mindful act that is developed over a lifetime. Having a list of standards provides us with an overview, but everything that contributes to the day to day life of a teacher cannot be codified in such a general way as much of it is specific to context.

THE iNFLUENCE OF WORLD ViEWS

An important consideration when trying to explore the territory in any profession is the influence of individual world views. This refers to the 'go to' ways in which we interpret aspects of life. Our world view is established in a number of ways: through education, culture, family, religion and the people we interact with regularly, and it encompasses perceptions, judgements, attitudes and norms of behaviour. It can even have an influence over our tastes and interests. At an individual level our world view is revealed by the values we choose to adopt and the ways in which these influence us. It could be described as a lens through which we see things (and don't see things), how we get around in the world and how we relate to others. This goes beyond perception but does of course have a big influence on how we perceive. A world view is really a set of core beliefs about aspects of 'reality' that informs thinking, knowing and doing, so some people might refer to it as their philosophy of life, their outlook or their mindset, the core elements of which are influenced by:

- Anthropology – the nature and purpose of man in general

- Aixology – beliefs about what is good and bad, right and wrong

- Epistemology – our beliefs about the nature of knowledge.

Figure 2.2   World view

In addition, we will be influenced by our beliefs about God, the nature of the universe and meta-physics – or the ultimate nature of reality. All of that is a lot to take in and really gives an impression of how much and by how many things we are influenced. In a nutshell: 'We don't see things as they are, we see them as we are' (anonymous).

In our professional roles, these factors will have a significant impact on how we conduct day to day activities. They will influence how we interact with learners, with colleagues and how we view our managers. This in turn structures behaviours and actions and influences our professional practice by informing:

- What we see as important

- What we consider less important

- How we view learning and subsequently how we plan teaching

- How we respond to events.

In a sense it provides the meaning we give to our work and shapes our practice – a little like Foucault's ideas about episteme – creating a set of fundamental assumptions that ground actions and are so basic they are almost invisible (Foucault, 1966). In Foucault's view, all thinking is centred around 'rules' which restrict our range of thought based on representations of reality – in other words, maps. This of course raises the question as to whether these maps are representative of the world outside our minds – do they show the territory? And if we are able to uncover the rules of maps – are we likely to discover new things? At first glance these may seem like somewhat fanciful ideas that belong in the realms of philosophy, the musings of those who have a lot of time to sit and ponder – but it is surprising how much of an influence such assumptions have on our practice and on what we do every single day.

CASE STUDY

Suki felt blessed that her education had provided her with a solid basis from which to develop her teaching role. She had been very successful in her academic career, passing all assessments with flying colours and racking up an impressive collection of accolades. In her view, this was convincing evidence that the schooling she had received was the answer to the problems many young people were facing today. She wanted to share what had worked so well for her and therefore modelled her professional practice on her own teachers. It had worked so well for her it was surely a recipe for success. The positive results Suki had been expecting from this did not materialise and she began to wonder what was wrong with her students.

It would seem that Suki's beliefs about learning came from her own experiences as a student; indeed modelling teaching on the way we were taught is not an uncommon strategy, so this is probably a safe assumption. But why wasn't this working in the way Suki had expected? Of course, we can't really answer that because we don't have all of the contextual information surrounding this case study and that is perhaps the most pertinent point. Suki was using her assumptions about teaching, based on her experiences of learning to judge how she should teach a group of learners – who (to state the obvious) were not her, and didn't have her previous experience so were working in an entirely different context. She had not taken into account the contextual details relating to her own teaching and had missed one of the key components of great teaching: *Get to know your learners.*

World view shapes the meaning teachers give to their work as well as the ways in which they undertake it. One of the key influencers in how we choose to structure our teaching comes from how we view learning – when most people think about planning a lesson there are two main considerations: what students are required to learn and the best strategies to help them do that.

ACTIVITY

The following list is based on words often used to describe what learning is. Select ten things from the list, then reduce this to your top five. If you feel very confident about this activity, you could then rank the top five in order of which most closely describes your view of learning.

Discovering	Understanding	Imagining
Applying	Doing	Developing skills
Remembering	Experimenting	Achieving
Evolving	Questioning	Knowing
Reasoning	Explaining	Gaining knowledge
Inducting	Deducting	Progressing
Receiving	Studying	Enlightenment

What does this tell you about your understanding of learning? It may be worth exploring this idea a little further by discussing it with a colleague or friend, or, getting down some thoughts in a reflective journal. Learning is a word we take for granted but it is used (and understood) in different ways. To give an example of that – consider the following definitions:

Learning is:

- 'a process by which we transform problematic frames of reference (mindsets, habits of mind, meaning perspectives) – sets of assumptions and expectations – to make them more inclusive, discriminating, open, reflective and emotionally able to change' (Mezirow, in Illeris, 2009: 92)

- 'any process that in living organisms leads to permanent capacity change and which is not solely due to biological maturation or ageing' (Illeris, 2007: 3)

- 'remembering, using and evaluating knowledge and skills to enable changes in perspective and behaviour' (Thompson and Wolstencroft, 2021: 131)

- '[observational] through modelling: from observing others one forms an idea of how new behaviors are performed, and on later occasions this coded information serves as a guide for action' (Bandura, 1977: 22)

- 'a process that is often not under our control and is wrapped up with the environments we inhabit and the relationships we make. It involves encountering signals from the senses; attending to them; looking for connections and meaning; and framing them so that we may act' (infed.org, online).

The only consistent thing within these definitions is that learning is viewed as a process, but what specifically that process is has not been clearly defined. Reference is made to transformation and change, to remembering and using knowledge. Some definitions explore how we learn, for example through problem solving, evaluation, observation and making connections. So, in all of this we are involved in a number of activities such as:

- Making sense or creating meaning
- Memorising or storing information

- A quantitative increase in 'knowledge' (another subjective word)

- Interpreting our experiences

- Changing behaviours.

Despite the popular use of the word, defining 'learning' does seem to be problematic: 'Questions about learning are addressed in virtually all areas of psychology. It is therefore surprising to see that researchers are rarely explicit about what they mean by the term' (De Houwer, Barnes-Holmes and Moors, 2013 online).

Learning is an individual and quite complex process and, counterintuitively, often something we do without thinking about it too much. Recent research around the topic even suggests that very little learning actually comes from deliberate teaching but has more to do with participation in life: 'Children learn by watching and imitating the people around them (observational learning) and they learn by listening to what other people say about how the world works – 'learning from testimony' (Gopnik, 2016: 89).

Taking all of this into account – how are we supposed to view learning? Whilst we acknowledge the likelihood that much of our learning does not come from formalised situations such as classrooms, some of it most certainly does and the teacher's impact on this is very important. What is interesting is that the complexity of learning is readily accepted, yet the act of teaching seems to have been diminished to a set of simple principles leading to standardised forms of practice. The process of becoming a teacher involves challenging some of this to make sure that *your* practice is the best practice for *your* learners and not simply 'best practice' as suggested in a simple map of teaching. In our view this is also a key component of great teaching. A first step in doing this is to establish what learning means to you.

REFLECTiON

Look back at the definitions you have been given in this chapter, explore a few more and think about your own experiences as a learner. Then commit to paper your answer to 'What is learning?'

When you have established your view on what learning is, it is worth turning your attention to how this might influence your view on teaching. In Chapter 1 we discussed differing views on the purpose of education. A belief about the purpose of education, coupled with views about what learning is, provides the basic ingredients for how we begin to frame our approach to teaching, so it is important to give some thought to this. Consider the examples in Table 2.1.

How does your view compare to any of the ones outlined in Table 2.1? Think about the similarities and differences, and what this tells you about what has influenced your view of teaching.

LESSON MAPS

Your approach to teaching is likely to have been influenced by your initial teacher training. Within this you are likely to have been introduced to a range of theories about learning, strategies for

Table 2.1 Examples of teaching approaches

Beliefs about learning	Translation in practice
Ben believes that learning is the developing of skills and the purpose of education is to provide people with the skills they need for employment.	Ben's lessons have a focus on applying knowledge in a given setting. He provides lots of examples of where learning is useful in the workplace and shares lots of hints and tips which worked for him in his previous career.
Suki believes that learning is about achieving qualifications as these provide evidence of achievements and capability.	Suki focuses her lesson on learning outcomes and how these will be translated in assessments. She feels that students need to know what assessors are looking for and that this information should be shared openly.
Marcus believes that learning is about questioning and that the purpose of education is to develop curiosity.	Marcus encourages his students to be autonomous learners by thinking about what it is they want and need to know. He likes to take an individualised approach and uses goal setting as a way of doing this.

applying these to teaching and maybe even something about the philosophy of education as a whole. You will also have been introduced to some standards, for example the Teachers' Standards for Qualified Teacher Status (QTS) or the Professional Standards for Qualified Teacher Learning and Skills (QTLS) (Department for Education, 2013). These very clearly make links to how you should plan for teaching:

Teachers' Standard 4 – Plan and teach well-structured lessons

Professional Standard 4 – Be creative and innovative in selecting and adapting strategies to help learners to learn.

Knowing where to start in planning can be difficult – it is a bit of a chicken and egg type of question. Do we start with the outcome – i.e., the intended learning for a lesson, or do we start by discovering the landscape – what is it that learners currently know and need to know? Is teaching about clear instruction or is it a journey of discovery? Who should decide what the learning outcomes of a lesson are – the teacher or the learners? Something often used to support the development of planning skills are templates for planning lessons such as the 'five minute lesson plan' (https://www.teachertoolkit.co.uk/5minplan/) or the diamond lesson plan (http://www.collegenet. co.uk/plans/diamond-lesson-plan). These are very useful frameworks when you are starting out but remember they are simply maps – part of the process of becoming a teacher is finding a planning strategy that works for you and your teaching context. Planning itself is not something that will go away as your experience develops, nor should it, but it is a thought process and templates are simply tools which can form a part of this.

In addition to planning templates, you may also have received guidance about teaching considered to be 'evidence-based', for example, the perfect lesson for Ofsted, which suggests a list of important criteria to address and the order to address them in. Such guides can easily be found online and often find their way into schools and colleges as forms of preferred practice. They normally look something like this:

- Have a starter activity (to stimulate curiosity and prepare the brain for learning)

- State your objectives (make them measurable and link them to Blooms Taxonomy of Learning – usually this is in the cognitive domain)

- The main body of the lesson needs to have a good pace; include lots of activities for formative assessment, keeping students motivated and on task, with differentiated activities to develop generic skills such as literacy, numeracy and ICT. It should also have a range of activities, choice of tasks for the learners and include single and group-based activities.

- Review the learning (which usually means going back to the objectives).

Whilst there is nothing inherently wrong with such guidelines (indeed they can be very helpful to new teachers) there is something quite disconcerting about how they are inculcated into practice as if 'real teaching' wouldn't happen without them. Such guides should provide a structure to inform your planning but they should not be doctrines to be slavishly followed. Any such guide is generic, which means that it cannot and should not fit every teaching scenario. The focus on learning in the cognitive domain is an example of this – what does this say about our understanding of vocational teaching (much of which will involve the development of psychomotor and affective skills). Is it more important when training a hairdresser that they can discuss the basics of cutting hair or that they can manipulate the scissors in the right way to be able to demonstrate this? We suspect we know which most customers would prefer. Many of the guides provided are understandably general in nature and for this reason are based on the most common teaching scenarios – this usually means they reflect the National Curriculum and the teaching that happens in schools – not always a good fit for other settings.

More recent literature, based on a range of research, does seem to be moving away from the generic approach and suggests that the focus of teaching should be on its impact on learning: 'It cannot be defined by compliance to a particular set of practices, however soundly based, nor by the demonstration of specific skills – nor, even, by the possession of particular teacher mindsets or understandings. Teaching is complex' (Coe *et al.*, 2020: 10).

Within this evidence review, four characteristics are outlined for great teachers:

1. understand the content they are teaching and how it is learnt

2. create a supportive environment for learning

3. manage the classroom to maximise opportunity to learn

4. present content, activities and interactions that activate their students' thinking.

(Ibid: 15)

This leads us to another key component of teaching: Treat guides and templates as maps, they are not the territory.

PROFESSIONAL AGENCY

In Chapter 1 we introduced the idea of professional identity, referring to the values, beliefs and self-concept assigned to the role. For many teachers this seems to be a problematic concept, muddied not only by external pressures but also by how the role is viewed by others. To illustrate this we would like to share a personal story.

I was at a meeting with a mortgage advisor trying to finalise the documentation for the purchase of my new house. As expected, there were questions about income and job role and one that stuck in my mind was a tick box where you had to choose what category your job role fitted into – something along the lines of:

Operative

Skilled

Administrative

Technical

Professional

I thought this was an interesting question and honestly had never really thought about my job in this way before. So I decided it might be a good idea to debate the listings – and my question to prompt this was: 'How do you define professional?' The advisor's response was something along the lines of: 'Well it's the type of training you do for your job … for example, my boyfriend is an electrician, he had to do quite a long training for his job, so he would fit in the professional category.' She then added: 'Shall we go for the next one down?' And that was it, in an instant, the role I had worked really hard to achieve and (contrary to the belief of the mortgage advisor) had actually undertaken quite a lot of training for, was dismissed with the flick of a pen!

In 2012, the then Secretary of State for Education, Michael Gove announced that QTS would not be required for teachers in academy schools and in 2013 the Government revoked the requirement for FE teachers to have formal teaching qualifications. There was understandable concern about these changes, particularly in terms of how this might 'de-professionalise' the status of teachers. How would others view the role if you didn't need a qualification to do it? But the story above suggests that there is much more to de-professionalisation than this.

The rise in standardised practice in education, resulting in what might be considered a more technical approach to teaching, has also given rise to debates about whether teaching should be considered a craft or a profession. In contrast, the importance of standards of practice, being a member of a professional body (such as the Chartered College of Teaching) and recognition given to a 'licence to practice' suggest that teaching differs very little from any other profession. There are entry requirements, the training is closely managed and there is little doubt that the impact of teaching is significant in both social and economic terms. The craft or profession debate which usually focuses on the requirement for professional (knowledge-based) judgement and the use of skills, might also be considered a little out of date. After all, don't all professions require elements of skill? A surgeon with a high level of practical skill might be preferable to one with an abundance of knowledge but lacking dexterity, yet there is no question in anyone's mind that this role fits into the category of 'profession'. Obviously, surgeons require skills and they also need an in-depth knowledge of anatomy and physiology so that they know where to cut! Teachers need to be skilled in how they manage groups of learners and how they create learning experiences. They also need the background knowledge to inform this – knowledge such as how learning happens and how learners respond to the learning experience, and yet whether their role is professional or not is in debate. Some might argue that one role deals with life and death situations and the other doesn't – that is true, but both have a significant impact on the quality of life and individual experiences.

What is important is whether or not teachers identify as professionals and if they do, how they develop and grow this professional identity. For teachers, this has been complicated by the changing ways in which the role is viewed in society and by the various changes that have been made to the regulation of teachers' qualifications and professional status. During training we don't often explore how we identify as professionals but during the process of being a teacher this is an important consideration.

Figure 2.3 Professional identity

Professional identity and agency are closely connected. As discussed in Chapter 1, professional identity refers to how we relate to the profession overall, rather than to a specific job role. There are many views on the meaning of agency – Friere (1970) saw it as something linked to collective action, whereby people engendered social empowerment, whilst others see it as attached to a role where it is focused on: 'the way in which actors critically shape their responses to problematic situations.' (Biesta and Tedder, 2006:11). Our view is that agency, whilst often situated in practice, is personal to individuals and takes the form of personal autonomy which informs action. For teachers, agency (or lack thereof) is very much influenced by factors outside of their immediate control. There are many stakeholders in education and it is an area of work subject to much policy influence. The impact of this sometimes makes teachers think they have no or very little agency, so it is perhaps something that must be claimed?

Professional agency is fundamental because it means teachers have some input in the construction of their work; it is also essential for ongoing creativity and innovation as well as motivation and well-being. Agency is an essential component of professional identity and that is something we need to construct for ourselves – someone else cannot tell you in what ways you identify with a role.

Figure 2.4 outlines the influence of workplace cultures and the profession itself over agency, illustrating how our sense of agency might be influenced by the things we are taught or experience in the professional role as well as the cultures within the individual organisations we work in.

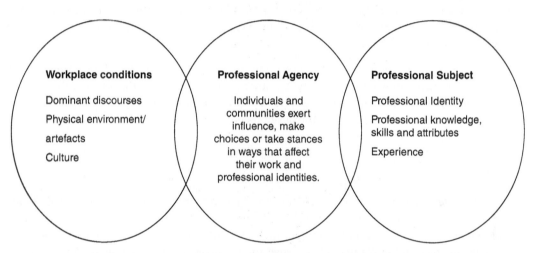

Figure 2.4 *Agency and identity (adapted from Estelápelto et al., 2014)*

CASE STUDY

Edvin had just begun working with a new team on a course he had taught in a previous college. It was one of his favourite areas and he had loads of ideas about how he could contribute to the team. The course was taught across a number of sites, so the team worked closely together to ensure some consistency. He had seen the resources the current team were using and knew that much of the work he had done in his previous role would be really helpful in updating and enhancing what was there - he was excited about the prospect! He spoke to a colleague about this and was told that he would have to put any ideas to the team leader. He did this and was told that the team could not make any changes for this academic year as the materials were already prepared. Undeterred, Edvin suggested that he develop some of his ideas and test them out with his group,

(Continued)

(Continued)

then feed back to the team overall. He was told that this was not acceptable as his group would be having a different experience to the others. Edvin then suggested that, rather than making a complete change, he adapt the resources he had and perhaps change around the order of some of the topics. He was then told in no uncertain terms that he had to 'deliver' the unit in exactly the same way as everyone else, using the same resources and any changes must be requested in writing so that they could be reviewed by the rest of the team. Edvin then realised what 'some consistency' meant and began to lose enthusiasm for his ideas.

Have you ever experienced this level of control over your work? We both have but are pleased to say that, in our collective experience, this tends to be within certain teams rather than organisations as a whole. It can be soul-destroying to be full of enthusiasm for something and then have your ideas dismissed straight away but this does sometimes happen. What does this say about the level of agency within this particular team?

As illustrated by the case study, agency can be diminished by cultural factors within teams as well as by a range of organisational processes which restrict the freedom to experiment – but this doesn't mean that it can't be claimed at an individual level or with groups of other people. Being a teacher means that you have responsibility for the development of teaching and learning in general and within your subject, so it is important to develop your professional agency. Indeed, this is another component of great teaching: *Find and develop your professional agency*. The following five suggestions may help with this:

Get involved in a community of practice (CoP) – Lave and Wenger (1991) use the term 'community of practice' to describe the ways in which learning takes place through social interaction in collaborative groups based around common interests. CoPs offer an opportunity for members to collaborate through the sharing of knowledge and resources, as well as acting as a forum for discussing ideas. Often these are facilitated by professional bodies so it is worth exploring options with the Chartered College of Teaching or the Society of Education and Training (SET). There is more information on this in chapter 9.

Explore opportunities for continuing professional development (CPD) – there are obvious choices available within formal qualifications (most universities offer MA, MEd, EdD or PhD programmes) but if that is too large an undertaking consider an area where you want to develop skills and look for a short course in that.

Find a special interest group – there are a number of special interest groups within education. Many of these use Twitter as a forum for communicating with members so that might be a good place to start. First you need to decide what your particular areas of interest are – are you interested in digital technologies, supporting individualised learning, learning in a particular subject? There is probably a group to fit.

Become a reflective practitioner – during training reflective practice isn't always valued as much as it should be and often ends up becoming an additional task in a very busy time. However, it can be really beneficial for developing our understanding and gaining a sense of connectedness. The process involves an exploration of thoughts and actions and provides the scope to evaluate events – through reflection we can consider professional values as well as develop different understandings and approaches. We may even gain some real insights.

Get active in research – action research is a really useful strategy for testing out new ideas in a pragmatic way. It provides a structure for evaluating the things that we do, as well as trying out new approaches, and need not be a long process.

CHAPTER SUMMARY

This chapter has focused on how our world view might influence our beliefs and values in relation to the teaching role, which in turn impacts on our practice. We have discussed the importance of professional agency, how this helps to construct professional identity and gives us influence over the ways in which we work. We have also highlighted some key components of what we view as great teaching and with those in mind it might be useful to consider:

- How can you really get to know your learners and make sure that your teaching works for them?

- In what ways could you claim and develop your professional agency?

FURTHER READING

Coe, R., Rauch, C. J., Kime, S. and Singleton, D. (2020) *Great Teaching Toolkit: Evidence Review*. Available at: https://www.greatteaching.com/.

3

ALL TEACHING IS COMMUNICATION

In this chapter we will explore:

- How perceptions can influence communication
- How we can use compassionate communication to overcome barriers
- How communication is perceived differently by each person

INTRODUCTION

'When people talk, listen completely. Most people never listen' (Hemingway, 1967: 3). These words are both highly pertinent and slightly confusing when read. What does 'listen completely' actually mean? The initial assumption is that when we talk about communication and listening to what is being said, we are referring to the words we hear, but as we explore in this chapter, we will learn that communication is about far more than that. The words themselves are merely part of a myriad of things that make up communication. Any single communication is influenced by who says it, how they say it, when they say it, what they look like when they say it – and those are just starting points for analysing communication.

To start thinking about how we view communication and, in particular, how the relationship you have with the sender affects it, let's look at a case study and take you back to school.

CASE STUDY: THE POWER RELATIONSHIP

The power relationship

Imagine the scene. You are sitting in a mathematics class, it's not your favourite subject and the teacher is not helping. His voice is beginning to sound a bit like white noise to you, you are aware he is talking but nothing is going in. Your mind drifts to other matters. Abruptly your attention is drawn back to the lesson. The teacher is making all the verbal clues that suggest that what he is saying was important. His voice slows and drops in tone. Each point is emphasised:

> 'So please remember this as it is important for your examination ... s is always equal to "ut" + half of "at" squared'. (Editor's Note: In case you are interested, this equation is the second law of motion and is used to calculate the distance an object has travelled)

Furiously you write down the equation and underline it to emphasise the importance of this bit of information. As you finish, the teacher calls your name and aims a question at you; he is asking you what 's' is equal to. Glancing down you repeat the equation; satisfied, the teacher nods, pleased you have got the answer right.

Clearly transmission of information has taken place with transfer from an initial source occurring and a receiver grasping the key points and, on the face of it, this communication could be seen as a success. However, this would be a very superficial analysis of the communication.

THE POWER/INFLUENCE RELATIONSHIP

The first point to note is that this communication involved a *power relationship*. Willemyns, Gallois and Callan (2010) discussed how power affects your response to any communication and whilst when we say the word 'power' we might imagine a degree of coercion, in truth it is something more akin to influence rather than straight power. Influence suggests that the person communicating is changing behaviour (or adding knowledge) in a far more subtle way.

This relationship is not unique to teaching. Within the world of marketing, a central premise has always been that people will respond to certain stimuli, one of which is the opinion of someone in a position of influence. Instagram influencers such as Zara McDermott have used this to great effect, sending messages to their millions of followers, trying to convince them to dress in a certain way, use a particular brand or support a good cause. To a lesser extent this is what happens in education – the power relationship that exists in a classroom means that students are likely to be aware of the formal relationship between teacher and student and so might well respond when this is demonstrated (for example when being told to 'sit down' or 'complete an exercise') but, for learning to take place power is not enough; what is needed is a change in behaviour and that is where 'influence' comes in.

We suspect the answer was a bit of both and clearly the way you perceive this task is a very individual one and is influenced by your view of hierarchical relationships; also the extent to which you trust, respect and maybe even value the other person. However, let's try to understand the core concept from the above case study: the power relationship.

DECONSTRUCTING POWER AND INFLUENCE

In this example, the teacher's word appeared to be accepted without question and hence the communication might be viewed as downwards in nature. The teacher passed on information from a position of authority and the student failed to challenge what was presented. This indicated that it was the power relationship that was at the forefront of this interaction.

This is a very normal situation in UK schools and colleges and it is interesting to reverse things and think what would happen if it had been the student passing on information. The likelihood is that the teacher would challenge the student, asking them to justify their points or at least quote their source. At the heart of this is the power imbalance that is inbuilt into a teacher–student relationship. However, this is not the whole story. Whilst it is comparatively straightforward to pass on information to students, such as the equation in our case study, to gain deeper understanding, and maybe the motivation to learn more, communication would need to influence the student to explore further rather than simply telling them the answer.

SHIFTING POWER

Please remember that power shifts constantly in a classroom and small moments can have a big change in how communication is perceived (Cornelius and Herrenkohl, 2004).

There are numerous examples of how power can shift. A teacher who handles a misbehaving student with panache can gain power in the eyes of a class, whilst one who fails to control students or loses their temper will lose power.

Returning to our maths case study, the communication appears to be transactional in nature. There is no attempt to put things in context and the point of this interaction appears merely to be to pass on information. What 's' actually means is not something that is explored, instead it is the equation that is stressed. Given the aforementioned power relationship between the teacher and the student, the focus on remembering an equation is what the student will take away from this lesson. This means that the purpose of this communication is to pass on something to students. As they have apparently received the information, then the transaction appears to be a success.

Finally, the contrast between the importance of the equation and the rest of the lesson is an important facet to note. It was the teacher that signalled the importance to the class, but it is also the case that communication is not just a one-way process. It is very easy to blame the teacher for the fact that everything else became 'white noise' but it is also the case that students need to play their part in effective communication.

THE ENVIRONMENT IN WHICH WE COMMUNICATE

Up to now we have focused on the human relationship when communication takes place. Power and influence has been assumed to be a product of two (or more) people communicating but there are other factors to consider. As we see in our next case study, communication does not exist in a vacuum.

CASE STUDY

The environment and communication

Another lesson, this time one that you enjoy. The teacher is enthusiastic, she encourages you to explore new areas of the curriculum and always listens when you have any problems. The topic she has introduced today is one that you have been looking forward to for most of the year and today should be a lesson that you throw yourself into.

It should be but isn't. Throughout the lesson your mind has been elsewhere. Your free Netflix trial expires tonight and you must remember to cancel it or you will be charged. You worry that if you say anything to the teacher then they might not take you seriously, or they might even laugh that you are worrying over such a trivial thing in your life. But you know that money has been very tight in your family recently and the importance of cancelling before you are charged is weighing heavily on your mind.

You look around; everyone else has packed up and is wandering over to the door. The teacher, looking perplexed, is clearly wondering why you are still in the classroom. The whole class has finished and the vast majority has passed you by.

DEALING WITH NOISE

In his description of how messages are transmitted from sender to receiver, Schramm (1955) makes reference to 'noise' which encompasses anything that stops you hearing the message. There could be physical constraints but noise might also be internal to yourself, which means that you are not focusing on the message. The concept has been much debated over the years but one thing that is difficult to argue with is the fact that environmental factors influence the success of any communication. It is certainly not the teacher's fault that you failed to engage with the lesson but for communication to truly work, it is vital that there is adequate preparation and the environment is taken into account. This might seem an obvious point; after all, we are told from our initial teacher training to ensure that our lessons are flexible enough to both meet individual needs and also take into account outside factors when teaching – but with communication this is not always remembered.

PRECONCEPTIONS AND COMMUNICATIONS

As we discussed in the previous chapter, everyone sees things in a different way and so communication can be an intensely personal thing for each student (and indeed for each teacher). Picking up on both verbal and non-verbal clues can help you check that your message has been understood but it is also important to understand that everyone has inbuilt assumptions and biases that will influence how they perceive both the message and also the person delivering it.

As an example of this, think about the following scenario: The lights are dimmed and you settle back in your seat to watch the latest action hero strut their stuff at the cinema. The hero watches as the designated bad guy wreaks havoc in the opening credits, unable to stop his enemy. Only when the opening credits have rolled does he speak. *"You will pay for this"* he intones. His voice is projected into the auditorium, his face full of menace.

Before reading on, imagine this situation and think about how the voice would sound. For some it might be an American voice, someone following in the path trod by Charlton Heston or Sylvester Stallone. Other people might imagine a British actor, the latest James Bond or maybe someone with an accent most commonly found in places such as the East End of London or Glasgow. In many ways, it doesn't matter who you imagine, the point is that the line given is likely to be delivered by someone who fits your expectations. Now, let's flip things around and imagine whether the message would be as powerful if our hero had a strong West Country accent or if instead of being muscle bound and tanned, they were short and pasty skinned? If the answer to this is 'no' then think why that is the case – after all the words are exactly the same no matter who delivers them, but remember, communication is the sum of many parts, not just the words spoken.

ALL TEACHING IS COMMUNICATION

If the look, the image, the accent, the dress, the size or the overall appearance of a person affects our perception of them, then it clearly makes sense that it would also affect our reaction to any communication from them. This is what we mean when we say that all teaching is communication. It is not just about WHAT you say, it is also about HOW you say it and WHO you are. The first two are comparatively easy to control and to adjust if there is a problem with communication, but the final one is far more difficult to influence. The major reason for that is that whilst there will be some commonly held generalisations, for the majority of people, their perceptions will be individual to themselves.

As we have explored above, the position you occupy does influence the way in which your communication is perceived but the multitude of other factors means that communication can be very difficult to optimise when faced with a class of maybe 30 students, each of which has their own views and ideas.

Of course there are a few general principles that are important to follow. Choosing the right medium for communication is important and checking that the decoding of any message has been done successfully is also vital. The latter is particularly important when dealing with different cultures where gestures or words might have differing meanings. Remember too that you are judged by the way you look, the way you act, the way you sound and also the previous experiences of those who you are communicating with.

If this all sounds complicated then it is because it definitely is! You can't possibly meet the expectations of everyone in your class and so, rather than trying to keep everyone happy yourself, the key is to reverse things and get them to meet your expectations. In some ways, we do this at the start of an academic year as a matter of course when we reinforce class rules and stress what we see as important in our sessions, but for communication it is even more important that we prepare students for receiving the messages we are passing on.

COMPASSIONATE COMMUNICATION

The volume of messages that are given to students can sometimes mean that important points are lost, whilst messages that are not perceived as being relevant will also be quickly forgotten. One technique that has often helped teachers communicate effectively comes from Newberg and Waldman (2013) who talk about the value of *compassionate communication*. This stresses the importance of accepting the other person's point of view and making sure that you do not forget the important skill of empathy. Their work suggests that there are 12 parts to this and they represent a very good way in which we can illustrate how communication is central to all teaching:

12 PARTS OF COMPASSIONATE COMMUNICATION

1. Relax

2. Stay present

3. Cultivate inner silence

4. Increase positivity

5. Reflect on your deepest values

6. Access a pleasant memory

7. Observe non-verbal cues

8. Express appreciation

9. Speak warmly

10. Speak slowly

11. Speak briefly

12. Listen deeply

Newberg and Waldman (2013)

EXPLORiNG THE CATEGORiES OF COMPASSiONATE COMMUNiCATiON

1. Relax – without wanting to state the obvious, communication is about far more than just a verbal message and your whole approach to the class permeates through to the class. Think about meeting someone you know well: often you don't have to ask to know how they feel, it is obvious from their body language, their demeanour or their gestures. It is the same in the classroom; students can pick up on your mood and how you are feeling very easily, so developing techniques to relax when teaching works well both for your own stress levels and also for reassuring the class. Becker *et al.* (2014) explored how the teacher's mood impacted on the class and their conclusion was that in many cases the teacher's mood was mirrored, so although you don't want your students too relaxed, some degree of calm is generally a good thing for improving students' receptiveness to your message.

2. Stay present and **3.** Cultivate inner silence – in the occasionally rowdy atmosphere of a classroom these can be difficult steps to follow, but focusing on the room by shutting out everything else can be a very effective strategy in promoting positive communication. Goffman (1959) described how we all have both a back stage persona (what we are like when we are in our own environment, for example at home) and a front stage persona which we adopt when interacting with other people in a more public setting. By using the front stage persona as a way of maintaining calm, you can ensure your students are aware that you are totally engaged with them. This in turn sets the expectations for them. Remember, as the teacher you have the greater power here and how you approach the communication influences the students, so by engaging with them, you set that expectation.

4. Increase positivity – how we communicate and the 'spin' we put on our communication undoubtedly influences others and so a positive approach is likely to be reflected in the response that you get.

ACTIVITY

Think about two differing ways in which you might present an idea:

"You are not going to like this but ...."

"I have an interesting proposition that might be right up your street ...."

What message does each approach convey?

For most people, it is likely that the first pre-supposes that the audience will not be happy with the points being proposed whilst the second is structured in order to pique interest. Whilst authenticity of approach is vital (if something is indeed bad news, then to present it as good news is likely to result in a loss of credibility), adopting a positive approach is often reflected in the responses that you receive.

5. We would argue that every one of us will go into the classroom with biases formed from all sorts of previous experiences and how we view the world. This is not necessarily a bad thing, having a view on things means that we can encourage healthy debate and the old idea that teachers should always be neutral in everything they do is an outdated one. We are not suggesting that you expose your biases to the class, more that you embrace them and understand them. It isn't easy to maintain a neutral position about everything in the classroom (indeed you could argue that attempting to be neutral is a statement in itself). We all have our inbuilt biases and they will influence how we see things and in turn they will be visible when we communicate with others.

By acknowledging your biases and your values you can start to understand how they impact on how you communicate. As we mentioned in the previous chapter, the way you see things is not the only way of looking at things and if you acknowledge this then you can begin to think about what message your students hear as well as what you are actually saying.

6. Access a pleasant memory – the way we communicate is often a reflection of our inner thoughts and, again, it is often easy to pick up on how people are feeling, not just from their words but also from everything from body language to what they stress when speaking. Accessing a pleasant memory encourages positivity and also relaxes your non-verbal communication. Although it can be a difficult exercise to do, talking in front of a mirror or a video camera will enable you to think about what message you are putting across. Put yourself in the shoes of your students and think how they would view you.

7. Observe nonverbal cues – given that communication does not exist in a vacuum, we must be aware of our audience as well as how we are feeling. You would have been told numerous times in your training that what we teach is not always what students learn and the same is true with any form of communication. Sometimes this might be down to a problem with the method you are using but often the issues are with your audience. Some signs that people are not listening are obvious, but others are more subtle. A student might be sitting up straight and be looking at you but that does not necessarily mean that they are listening. Look for non-verbal clues such as whether they react to what you say. A delay in responding is often a clue that a student who looks superficially engaged is not necessarily listening.

8. Express appreciation – if we accept the premise that all teaching is communication then expressing appreciation, or at the very least acknowledging contributions, is essential. Many teachers struggle with this as it sometimes feels far too mechanical to simply say 'thank you' or 'good point' when a contribution is made, so it is often necessary to seek out alternative ways of expressing appreciation. Given the power that you hold as a teacher when communicating, the reaction of students is often linked to your position as well as how you show your appreciation. Some students do not seek verbal praise in front of their peers, indeed some actively discourage it, but that is not to say that they don't want (or deserve) appreciation. Communicating in a more subtle manner can be effective; this could be either non-verbal in nature or alternatively verbal praise delivered in private rather than in front of the whole class. By expressing appreciation you are often able to bring down barriers to communication as students are more willing to listen.

9. Speak warmly and **10.** Speak slowly – much is made of the idea of authentic communication and rightly so. False praise can be as destructive as ill thought-out criticism and so it is important to be clear with what you say, but also ensure that it is accurate and has a clear purpose. The speed of what you say is also important to be aware of; whilst speaking quickly can convey enthusiasm, it can be tricky to follow and sometimes when communication is important, slowing down can be a powerful tool.

11. Speak briefly – empathy is so important when we discuss communication and please always remember that processing communication can be tiring. Messages that are brief and are reinforced only when they are not fully absorbed are far more powerful than talking at length. Remember that everyone is different in how they prefer to communicate but a significant number of people prefer to do some of the work themselves.

12. Listen deeply – finally communication is a two-way process and focusing on the receiver is important. This is not to say that the receiver should drive the communication though. It is easy to react to the other person when practising listening and, whilst it is important to listen, it is also important to keep control of the communication and to ask relevant questions to fully understand what they are saying. Allow the other person to do the same and the likelihood is that clarity will come. An example of this became very apparent in the pandemic of 2020. In many educational establishments there has traditionally been an expectation that communications with students have been answered in 48 hours. If we contrast this to, maybe, a text message received from a friend that you might answer instantaneously, it is easy to draw the conclusion that the latter is clearly more important than the former. After all, if something is not responded to until 48 hours have passed, then the person asking the question might come to this conclusion. The reality of course is that the two situations are rather different. Most social interactions will only require a very brief amount of thinking, whilst work emails will need much deeper thought. However, to ensure that this is understood, everyone must be told.

CHAPTER SUMMARY

In this chapter we have attempted to move the narrative beyond seeing communication merely as a verbal transaction in order to explore its complexity. As discussed in the first two chapters, the way you see the world and your previous experiences have a direct impact on your communications with students, as does the perception of power within the teacher–student relationship. The 12-step plan for compassionate communication has been introduced as a framework to enhance your communication with learners and with this in mind, we would like to leave you with some questions for reflection:

- What aspects of communication are most challenging in your role?

- In what ways might compassionate communication enhance your communication with students?

 FURTHER READING

Chandler, D. (1994) *The Transmission Model of Communication.* Available at: http://visual-memory. co.uk/daniel/Documents/short/trans.html?LMCL=UucUH1.

4

UNDERSTANDING BEHAVIOUR

In this chapter we will explore:

- The idea that all behaviour has a positive intent
- Ways of managing our own behaviour
- How to create a positive classroom environment

INTRODUCTION

Teachers often fall into two camps when it comes to managing challenging behaviour – those who think they can control it and those who think they can't. This sounds like something of a sweeping statement and may suggest that if you fall into the latter category you might want to rethink your career, as there is little doubt that whatever phase of education you work in, there will always be times when you find behaviour within the classroom challenging. But do we really have any control over someone else's behaviour? Or do we simply influence it through the environment we create and the ways we interact? In this chapter we will discuss factors influencing behaviour and will explore the importance of managing our own behaviour in order to create a positive classroom environment.

MANAGING CHALLENGING BEHAVIOUR

Behaviour management is a hot topic in schools, colleges and even universities and there is a plethora of information about how we should address this challenge. It has been a focus for education stakeholders for some time and forms a key part of the Department for Education's Core Content Framework (CCF) for initial teacher education. The guidelines in the CCF stress that teachers should:

- Develop positive and safe classroom environments

- Be able to respond quickly to behaviour that threatens emotional safety

- Establish supportive and inclusive environments – with a predictable system of reward and sanction in the classroom

- Work alongside colleagues as part of a wider system of behaviour management

- Give manageable, specific and sequential instructions, checking understanding of instructions before instruction begins

- Establish effective routines and expectations.

(Department for Education 2019)

Figure 4.1   Core Content Framework

So far, so logical. Whilst there is nothing we would necessarily disagree with here, we do think that something is missing in this approach.

REFLECTION

Read the key bullet points from the CCF again and try to do this with a completely open mind. This might mean forgetting about everything you have been taught through teacher training and your organisation's behaviour policy. Just think about the points in relation to behaviour generally - any behaviour - whether it is at school, at home or in personal relationships. What does this tell you about the underpinning assumptions and beliefs about managing behaviour?

At first glance, these seem like very logical steps in managing classroom behaviour, but what informs them? There are two key influences here – the need for emotional (and I think we can assume, physical) safety and the need to monitor and address any challenging behaviour as it occurs. In essence this is based on a behaviourist approach as there is a focus on using a system of sanctions and rewards, thereby providing positive and negative reinforcement in order to encourage desired behaviours and discourage what is considered to be undesirable. This is not that unusual and is an approach that is advocated in many models of behaviour management.

"She just doesn't seem to get it ↳ I sit↳ she gives me a treat it's simple behaviourism theory!!"

Figure 4.2   Training

What seems to be missing from the outline in the CCF is any reference to trying to actually understand behaviour – the focus is on managing and monitoring. This may seem like a technicality but if we don't understand the reasons for what is happening then we may also apply the wrong strategy to managing it and ultimately that could result in even more undesirable responses! Anyone who has ever tried training a puppy will most certainly understand this – if you misinterpret what your dog is trying to tell you, and reward a behaviour when you should be correcting it, you will actually be reinforcing bad habits that are very difficult for your dog to unlearn. Similarly, if you punish when the best strategy is to ignore, you may start to create anxieties in your pet that could turn into unpleasant or aggressive behaviours. There is some recognition of this in 'The Great Teaching Toolkit 2020' which outlines the importance of promoting positive relationships with learners based on mutual respect as well as being sensitive to individual needs and emotions (Coe *et al.*, 2020).

SOME TYPICAL APPROACHES

Cowley's (2014) 7 Cs of behaviour management focuses on clear boundaries and clear expectations. This involves:
- Engaging students in the decisions
- Ensuring that positive behaviour management is used
- Using consequences rather than confrontation

Canter and Canter (2001): Assertive Discipline: This involves a high level of teacher control and:
- Assumption that students will misbehave
- Rewards which should be used to encourage good behaviour
- Consistency of approach
- The teacher having the final authority

Some key principles in these models:

- Two way process

- Clarity and consistency

- Roles in the classroom

Ford (2004) Responsible Thinking Process (RTP) a model of behaviour which includes:
- Students taking responsibility
- Stressing mutual respect
- Being non-punitive in nature

Rogers (2015) This model is based on the human nature of behaviour management, so stresses:
- Prevention is the best approach to take
- Consequences of poor behaviour should be stressed
- Non-confrontational approach
- Repair bridges when needed

Figure 4.3   Summary of behaviour management strategies

Often, discussions about how to manage challenging behaviour come from very different views, known as progressive and traditional. Those who espouse a traditional view tend to focus on a teacher centred approach to education whilst the progressive approach sees the teacher's role as one of facilitator. You are likely to have been taught a range of techniques in your teacher training that fit one or other of these views. Our role is not to tell you whether one approach is 'right' and the other 'wrong', that is for you to decide, but the debate tends to be polarising in nature so it is important to remember not to reject things simply because they don't fit with what you have been taught.

The four theories illustrated in Figure 4.3 are representative of current ideas in relation to managing classroom behaviour. Each outlines a different focus but the three themes central in the diagram are present in all of them.

Firstly, that behaviour management needs to be a two-way process. In its simplest form, the behaviourist approach that is at the heart of the CCF asks the teacher to create a stimulus (maybe something such as one of Cowley's 7Cs or Canter and Canters' rules) that will lead to a response. If the response is not present then the approach cannot work (Canter and Canter, 2001; Cowley, 2013). The necessity for a two-way process is more explicit in Ford's (2004) work and also in Rogers' (2015) work as they require the students to be part of the commitment to positive behaviour.

The second commonality is the need for clarity and consistency. Whilst this is a staple of teacher training books, it does have dangers attached to it. Whilst a commitment to a clear cause could be seen as admirable, the degree of clarity and (in particular) consistency in a classroom might well crumble for pragmatic reasons. Stating the obvious, you might well take a different approach to a high performing A level group than one that you would take with a younger, more rowdy class, so whilst clarity and consistency is a common theme, it does have to be treated with caution.

EVERY BEHAViOUR HAS A POSiTiVE iNTENT

There is always a reason behind why someone behaves the way they do, even if it is not in their conscious awareness at the time. The assumption that every behaviour has a positive intent acknowledges this by focusing attention on the underlying reasons for the behaviour, rather than the behaviour itself. By recognising the intent, we are far more likely to respond to the behaviour in a way that will engender a positive outcome.

As outlined in Chapter 2, we interact with the world based on our mental representations of it. Sometimes these representations are inaccurate; this can lead to distorted thinking and result in very specific beliefs which in turn lead to certain consequences. Our emotions and behaviours are not necessarily determined by life events but by our perception of events, and that is an important point to remember. Our assumptions aren't always correct and when assumptions are irrational, they may cause inappropriate behaviours and will in turn limit our chances of success. The ABC model of behaviour clearly sets out this idea (Ellis 1991):

A – Activating event (or antecedent) – this refers to a situation that is prompting the irrational behaviour.

B – Beliefs about the event – this is our personal interpretation and how we are creating meaning from a particular event.

C – Consequences of the event – specifically any negative feelings experienced. Ellis suggests that it is not the event itself that is the cause of negative emotions but the way in which it is interpreted – the irrational belief about it.

─────── CASE STUDY ───────

Luke is quieter than usual and doesn't seem to want to participate in the lesson. His teacher assumes he is struggling with the activity she has given out so she asks one of the other students to work with him. At this point, Luke gets up abruptly, knocks over his chair and shouting 'I am not doing this!' storms out of the room.

Luke's teacher is completely baffled. He is normally quite a diligent student and she can't understand this behaviour. She later discovers that Luke had failed an English test taken the previous week and had just received the results.

How might the ABC model apply in Luke's case? A possible antecedent to Luke's behaviour could be that he failed an English test and was feeling upset about that. This in turn could make him question his own ability, he may even have developed the belief that he is no good at English, or at tests or maybe even that he just isn't very bright. If this is the case then his teacher's well-meaning intervention may well have had the opposite effect, as it could have unwittingly helped to reinforce any negative beliefs he had generated about his abilities. The important point is that there will be a cause and for Luke there will be a positive intent behind his behaviour. By reacting in the way that he did, he could temporarily escape the negative feelings brought about by the incident.

For Luke's teacher however, there is no background information – all she sees is the actual behaviour and if that is her focus, then it is also quite likely that she will simply react to the incident. For her there may be a focus on what consequences there should be; after all, she doesn't want to give the impression to other students that this behaviour is acceptable. On the other hand, over-reacting can simply exacerbate the situation.

─────── REFLECTION ───────

If you were the teacher in this scenario, what potential actions could you take?

Clearly this is a very personal decision but there are a number of potential answers, including:

- a quiet word at the end of the class away from his classmates. This has the great advantage of moving the conversation from a confrontation to a conversation.

- asking colleagues about their experiences with Luke to see if this was an isolated occurrence. If there is a pattern of behaviour then it might require a specific intervention and the involvement of other members of the team/support staff.

- following it up with a personal tutor who may be able to offer further insights that would help develop an understanding of what had caused the outburst. Working with the personal tutor also means that information can be collated in one place, which will help if any formal intervention is needed.

- trying to establish if Luke requires any additional support, for example study skills or counselling and signposting to specialist staff who can provide this.

Others' behaviour can sometimes surprise us and it is very easy to focus on managing the outcome rather than trying to understand the cause. That is not to say that consequences such as storming out of the room should be ignored, but by focusing exclusively on the consequences, we run the risk of allowing the behaviour to be repeated as the antecedent is still in place. Think about behaviour in the same way you would think about weeds in your garden; the easy way out is to pluck out the sections that are visible, the more difficult part is to pluck out the root. However, this is necessary if you want all plants to grow in harmony.

POSSiBLE ANTECEDENTS TO CHALLENGiNG BEHAViOUR

Desire for power or recognition: As we discussed in Chapter 3, power is a key concept when communicating, even in the classroom. It is easy to assume that it is the teacher who sets the scene for the classroom and ensures that the lesson proceeds in the right direction, but this isn't always the case. Some learners can be dominant and sometimes they choose to behave in challenging ways just as a way of getting noticed. It is very easy to get 'lost' within a class, particularly in large groups. If you think back to when you were at school, how often were in you in groups of 20–30 students? How many of those people can you name? Aside from close friends, the likelihood is that you will only remember those who stood out. Perhaps they were always top of the class – or maybe they were the ones who gave the teachers a hard time, the class clown, the miscreants? The drive for recognition and the need to be seen as powerful can be a strong antecedent (Cothran, Hodges Kulinna and Garrahy, 2009).

Classroom environment: Our environment can have a significant influence on our behaviour. At one level that statement is so simplistic it barely needs to be stated. Inevitably, if you feel uncomfortable, are hungry, too cold or too hot, this is going to cause a distraction and there are many factors that teachers have little or no control over (for example buildings, classroom furniture etc.). However, one thing the teacher can influence is the social and emotional environment within the classroom:

> I've come to the frightening conclusion that I am the decisive element in the classroom. It's my personal approach that creates the climate. It's my daily mood that makes the weather. As a teacher, I possess a tremendous power to make a child's life miserable or joyous. I can be a tool of torture or an instrument of inspiration. I can humiliate or heal. In all situations, it is my response that decides whether a crisis will be escalated or de-escalated and a child humanized or dehumanized.

(Ginott, 1972: 15–16)

As suggested by Ginott, classroom environment goes way beyond practical factors and is most certainly influenced by the teacher's approach. Whilst it is tempting to focus on the content of your teaching, it is important to remember that the success of that teaching is very likely to be influenced by social and emotional factors. Illeris referred to this as the tension field of learning (Illeris, 2007), demonstrating the interplay between social, emotional and content aspects of lessons.

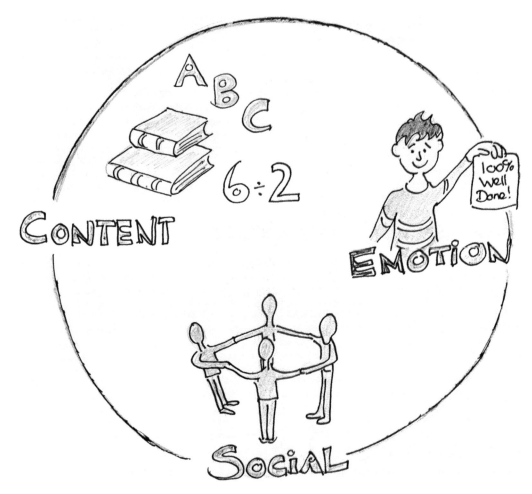

Figure 4.4   Tension field of learning

Unclear boundaries: The establishment of clear boundaries within the classroom is essential if we want to create a comfortable environment in which everyone feels safe. Whilst boundaries don't necessarily eliminate challenging behaviour they do provide clarity on what is generally considered acceptable. Having boundaries, usually articulated as classroom rules, simply means that we are working in an environment of openness and respect. This can be reinforced by taking a diplomatic approach to setting boundaries – by negotiating what is considered appropriate behaviour (or not) we also begin a dialogue about this important topic, which can be returned to when required.

Teaching matters: A successful lesson isn't just about managing learners' behaviour. It also requires good teaching. This means that the teacher needs to understand their subject and how it is learnt, they need to present content and have activities that will activate learners' thinking and they need to create a supportive environment in which this can happen (Coe *et al.*, 2020). Lessons work best when classes are well structured, capture learners' interest and can demonstrate relevance of the learning and not surprisingly, good lessons in which learners are engaged tend to have fewer issues with challenging behaviour.

MANAGiNG OUR OWN BEHAViOUR

As highlighted in the CCF guidelines, much of the focus in relation to managing behaviour seems to be on how teachers monitor and manage their learners' behaviours but this may well be the wrong focus. If we are to assume that every behaviour has a positive intent, then we may begin to look at learners' behaviours in a totally different light. In addition, we also need to consider our own behaviours and the impact they have on our learners. Ginott made a very significant point when he suggested that teachers have the power to make students' lives miserable or joyous.

Having a greater awareness of our own behaviour is helpful in all sorts of ways and is believed to support our relationships, well-being and happiness. It is also suggested that people with high levels of self-awareness feel more in control of life and have more personal growth (Harrington and Loffredo, 2010). It could be argued that understanding ourselves is the first step to managing our own behaviour in order to achieve the outcomes we want.

EMOTiONAL iNTELLiGENCE

The theory of emotional intelligence developed through studies of cognition, specifically the consideration of how emotions affect our thoughts and in turn our actions. It also involves the ways in which we assess emotions in ourselves and others (Salovey and Mayer, 1990). By developing our emotional intelligence we enhance our skill in managing our own emotions as well as positively influencing others, which in turn helps us to handle relationships smoothly (Goleman, 1996). An emotionally intelligent person is likely to display the following traits:

- An awareness of and ability to name their own emotions and express these in appropriate ways

- Ability to control emotions when communicating with others

- Ability to deal with conflict

- Ability to demonstrate integrity and engender trust from others

- Flexibility in their approach to other people and to life and ability to cope with change

- An awareness of their own strengths and weaknesses and ability to learn from mistakes

- Ability to give constructive feedback to others.

(Thompson, 2019)

In some ways emotional intelligence seems like a small piece of magic – we simply have to develop a few positive traits and all of our relationship worries will disappear. It will most certainly help in the development of more harmonious relationships; the difficulty is that processing and acting on emotions is a part of habitual behaviour patterns built up over years and in order to change those we also need to change the messages we have learnt to give ourselves. A key premise of Cognitive Behavioural Therapy (CBT) is that the way we think has a significant impact on our emotions and the way we respond to them; therefore, to develop emotional intelligence there are two things to focus on:

- Emotional literacy – our ability to express our feelings by recognising and naming emotions as well as our capacity to actively listen to and empathize with others.

- Channelling and applying emotions – thinking about the messages we give ourselves and learning to change our thoughts in order to change how we feel.

When you have grown up in a culture where discussing feelings is not necessarily encouraged, developing emotional literacy can be a challenge, but this does have a very clear purpose in enhancing our relationships with others. By developing emotional literacy we learn to effectively communicate our feelings and in doing so create clarity for ourselves and others. One way of doing this is to start sentences with 'I feel' and to try to do so without any justification. For example, 'I feel judged' rather than 'I feel that they are judging me'. Sounds simple enough but most of us are used to justifying our feelings – we try to find reasons for them and often those reasons include allocating blame to others. This is particularly true when they are considered negative feelings like 'sad' or 'scared'. Growing up we are often encouraged to ignore those things, told to 'look on the bright side' or 'there is nothing to be scared of'. Whilst this may be true, it also begins a pattern of negating unpleasant emotions. The feelings of course don't simply disappear; instead we find different ways of escaping them. Rather than acknowledging and feeling our emotions we might choose to block them with a range of other things like excessive busyness or obsessing about something unrelated. According to Burns (2020), every negative feeling results from a specific negative thought, so if we simply cover the thought with another activity, the feelings will be resurrected when the blocking activity ends. A strategy to overcome this is to develop the ability to 'reckon with' our emotions (Brown, 2015), acknowledge them and get curious about how the feelings connect with our behaviour.

CHANNELLING AND APPLYING EMOTIONS

Emotions have a very practical purpose in our lives; for example, love encourages us to connect with others and fear can keep us safe. However, if we believe that thoughts are inextricably linked to our emotions, that also means that the emotions themselves are subject to interpretation and misinterpretation. This is why getting curious about them is so important. When we ignore our emotions they are never fully acknowledged and can fester into something negative. Like a neglected plant, instead of being allowed to grow and blossom they develop a dried up, twisted appearance that we would rather not see. The Triple Column technique is a strategy for exploring negative thoughts and enhancing objectivity in thinking so that our thoughts don't dissolve into unhelpful behaviours. It is a reflective tool that provides the scope to identify a situation, record our feelings about it and then look for any distortions in how we are thinking about it.

ACTIVITY

Try this for yourself. Think about your teaching over the last week; are there any events that have caused you to feel negative? Then complete the triple column to establish your thoughts and potential distortions. All you need is three columns with the headings, 'automatic thoughts', 'distortions', 'rational responses'. We have included an example from our practice to get you started (see Table 4.1).

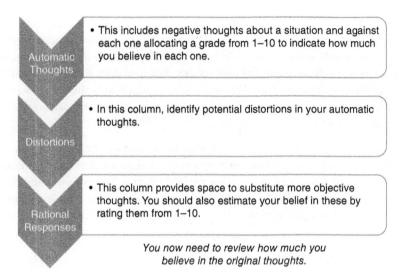

Figure 4.5   Triple column technique (adapted from Burns, 1990)

Table 4.1   Example triple column entry

Automatic thoughts	Distortions	Rational responses
My online lecture this week was a bit flat! It was with students I don't know and I didn't get much interaction from them. I obviously didn't make the content very exciting (9) If they were interested they would have interacted more and asked some questions (8) I must be boring as a lecturer! (8)	Because the group didn't know me it is possible they were not as confident about interacting or asking questions (9) Actually they all stayed to the end - they could have logged off early - maybe that suggests some interest? (7) Even if the lecture was a bit boring ... that doesn't make me a boring lecturer (10)	Lack of knowledge of the students is probably a factor here ... maybe I should have got more information about them? (10) It is possible that some of the audience were bored but as they stayed and there was some interaction, they must have found some of it interesting (9) You are not your last lecture ... you can do better next time (10)

An important aspect of enhancing emotional intelligence is increasing self-awareness: 'To know thyself is the beginning of wisdom' (attributed to Socrates). This of course includes aspects of ourself that are not as open, as well as those we would rather stayed hidden. In these instances, the aim is to view things more objectively by practising authenticity. But how does all of this help our teaching? As Rogers said all those years ago: 'The only person who is educated is the person who has learned how to learn: the person who has learned how to adapt and change; the person who has realised that no knowledge gives a basis for security' (Rogers, 1969: 152).

By continuing developing self-awareness we are also developing our understanding of others. The techniques that work for you in encouraging behaviour change are also the techniques that will work for your learners. Not only will you develop better understanding of how your behaviour influences those around you, you will also develop more insight into why you find some behaviours challenging. You may also begin to look at them more objectively which will help you to find the right intervention.

Within any classroom it is important to develop a climate of mutual respect, and to do this authentically we should also consider ways in which to:

- provide opportunities to reflect on feelings
- acknowledge and articulate emotions
- seek out strategies for managing behaviours that don't serve us
- observe others modelling positive behaviours.

The strategies you use to develop this will vary depending on the learners you are working with. Adult learners, for example, could be encouraged to keep reflective logs or get involved in thought-provoking discussion. Younger learners might be involved in creating posters or playing games. Whilst it is important that activities are age appropriate, this is often down to how they are used rather than the activity itself; for example we have used poster creation for adult learners to explore their own behaviour in the classroom (yes, adults can also exhibit challenging behaviour!) and have used stories to prompt alternative ways of thinking about things. Equally we have seen pupils in primary school conduct very grown-up discussions.

REFLECTION

Think about some strategies you could implement to create an emotionally intelligent classroom. How might these things influence learners' behaviour in a positive way?

CREATING A POSITIVE CLASSROOM

When talking about behaviour management the mistake many people make is to focus solely on a defined number of strategies in the belief that this will solve problems. Of course strategies are important for dealing with incidents as they occur, but it is important that you look at the wider picture. To illustrate this point, think about the difference between homeopathy and more mainstream medicine. If you go to your local GP, the likelihood is that they will diagnose what is wrong with you, prescribe a solution and only rarely will they ask anything about underlying issues. This is for a variety of reasons, not least a lack of time. The principles of homeopathy revolve around the fact that you look at the whole person rather than merely addressing the visible problem. In this way, homeopathists believe that you are able to prevent future occurrences as well as making sure that the body is in balance.

In many ways the creation of a positive classroom mirrors a combination of all of the factors that we have discussed in this chapter and so it is a folly to merely focus on one. Remember our central message is that all behaviour has a positive intent and establishing a positive classroom is a key part to this.

It goes without saying that creating a positive classroom environment is a key component of managing challenging behaviour. Perhaps the most important aspect of this is that students feel safe – both physically and emotionally. Here are a few things to think about:

- Do your students believe that you care about them? Remember to ask yourself – do you know the names of all your students? Have you noticed any changes in behaviour for any of your classes? Could you write a short pen portrait of each person in your class? If the answer to all these questions is 'yes' then you can be pretty sure that you are demonstrating care.

- What happens when one of your students makes a mistake or gets a question wrong? A positive classroom environment allows students to make mistakes, so it is important that your reaction gives the impression that mistakes are a crucial part of learning. It is also important that you think about how the other students react and manage any inappropriate responses. Respect must be shown to everyone and everyone's opinions should be valued – this is key to generating a feeling of safety.

- What additional forms of support are there in your class? In a large group it is important that students feel supported, not just by you but by their peers (as well as any support workers that are in the classroom), so think about how students react if one of their number needs help. A strong sense of community in a class can be of immense support to your students … and to you!

- How do you model positive attitudes and values? Modelling is a really effective strategy for influencing behaviour as it provides an immediate template for others to follow. Modelling is really about practising what you preach, so if you have certain expectations of learners, for example not interrupting when others are speaking, then of course the same rule applies to you. It is easy to underestimate the power that teachers have to influence others' behaviour simply by managing their own.

- Have you instilled a focus on emotional intelligence in your teaching? For this to happen you need to consider how you provide opportunities for learners to reflect on and articulate their feelings and how, at an individual level, learners can seek out strategies to help them manage the behaviours that are not serving them.

CHAPTER SUMMARY

In this chapter we have focused on the idea that all behaviour has a positive intent. The adoption of this phrase as a focus was to stress the importance of understanding behaviour before we try to manage it. Whilst there is no doubt that developing a range of strategies to help us manage challenges when they arise is one of the most useful skills teachers will learn, it is also important to recognise the influence our own behaviour has on others. It could be argued that managing our own behaviour and building our emotional intelligence is a pre-requisite to addressing challenges in the classroom. At the beginning of the chapter we considered the idea that teachers tend to fall into two camps when it comes to managing or controlling behaviour – those who think they can and those who think they can't. If you happened to fall into the second category this probably bodes well for your ability to effectively deal with challenges in the classroom. It is our belief that it is not possible to control others' behaviours – the only thing we have control over is ourselves and for that reason we have stressed the importance of enhancing awareness of our own behaviours as well as building our skills in emotional intelligence so that we can not only empathise with others but can have a positive influence on their interactions within a group. With that in mind there are two questions for you to reflect on:

- In what ways do you influence the behaviour in your classroom?

- How might you develop an emotionally intelligent classroom?

 FURTHER READING

Goleman, D. (1996) *Emotional Intelligence: Why It Can Matter More than IQ*, London: Bloomsbury.

5

FLEXIBILITY IS KEY

In this chapter we will explore:

- The rise in formulaic approaches to teaching
- The importance of taking a flexible approach
- Strategies for increasing your flexibility

iNTRODUCTiON

Teaching is a creative, relational role that requires the ability to adapt to a range of situations. Even the most detailed planning cannot hope to prepare us for every eventuality, so it is important that we develop flexibility not only in our responses to what is going on around us but also in our thinking. Flexibility could be defined as the ability to bend or stretch easily in order to adapt to changes in our situation and in a way that is what we are talking about, although our focus is more on the ability to think in a range of different ways in order to meet the demands of our professional lives. As discussed in Chapter 4, we don't have the power to control other people or events, but we are able to control our responses to them, and developing our range of responses means we will have more choices. In this chapter we will discuss the importance of being able to adapt our professional practice and our thinking in order to increase the range of choices available to us as well as increase our ability to influence change.

THE RiSE iN STANDARDiSED APPROACHES TO TEACHiNG

In Chapter 1 we outlined some of the historical events which have influenced teaching today and in Chapter 2 we explored some of the practical ways this has shaped professional practice. On the surface, having recommended teaching approaches can seem quite innocent, even useful and time-saving, but when embedded into a culture in which practice is driven by a plethora of 'shoulds' and 'musts', formulas for teaching can also be suffocating. The real danger is not in the approaches themselves but in the evolution of a very narrowly defined view of what 'good' teaching is, especially when this becomes embedded into practice in such a way that it is beyond question.

Figure 5.1   One size fits all

Hegemony relates to the dominance of particular beliefs that are often dictated by powerful influencers such as government departments or professional bodies. In a professional context this is represented by what is considered to be 'the right way to do things' and is underpinned by technical rationalism (Schön, 1983). This is an approach to teaching which sees practice as being quite generic so that approaches to it are similar regardless of content. This tends to favour the use of formulas and the application of simple solutions to problems. It could be described as a 'one size fits all' approach. In theory this is logical as formulas tend to be clearly structured and easy to follow, so this approach can seem very attractive but can also lead to the application of generic practice, which is not always applicable in specific contexts. A typical example of this might be the accepted practice of sharing learning objectives with students at the beginning of the lesson and then checking them regularly throughout the lesson. It is debateable whether or not this actually enhances students' ability to learn, but is so embedded it has become a rule. But what if a teacher's learning objectives are limiting the lesson? What if learners could actually achieve much more than the teacher thought they could? Often, popular ideas about teaching are drawn from a research base and are well publicised by those with influence. That certainly adds a level of gravitas which can be difficult to argue with; nevertheless we need to be wary of dualistic thinking, the kind of either/or thought that does not take into account contextual detail, and this means we need to constantly challenge current thinking – including our own!

CASE STUDY

Astrid loves her job. She works in an FE college with young adults who have a range of physical and learning disabilities. Her role is varied and includes helping her learners develop their communication skills as well as teaching them a variety of subjects. Each day is as different as each learner's ability and needs. It is a very challenging but rewarding job and Astrid is committed to doing it to the best of her ability, so attends every available training event in order to continue her own learning. Recently she attended a workshop on 'the grade one lesson plan', which, given the college's focus on Ofsted, seemed appropriate. She also knew that her manager wanted to implement standardised planning across the department, so thought she would get a step ahead. One of the aspects of the workshop she was struggling with was writing specific learning objectives. The workshop leader was very specific about what was and wasn't acceptable. When she explained her setting and the difficulties associated with measuring learning at anything other than an individual level, she was told to write objectives that everyone could achieve. On reflection, Astrid realised this would mean making the objectives so simple that they wouldn't challenge individual learners and one of her own beliefs was that learners, whatever their ability level, should be challenged. It was a dilemma!

It can feel quite daunting to question current wisdom on teaching, particularly when you first start in the profession, but to become a successful teacher it is important to constantly check that what you are doing will lead to the best outcomes for your learners. In Astrid's case, the setting of what she viewed as trite learning objectives, just to meet the needs of a pro-forma for planning lessons, was certainly something to be challenged. Her learners (as with most groups) have diverse needs and generic objectives would not be the best way to challenge them. The result of applying this approach would be that she would have to set very easy objectives so that everyone could achieve them and that was something that challenged her core values about teaching.

THE IMPACT OF FORMULAIC PRACTICE

Every school and college in the country is driven by the need to ensure they are producing good results and each one will have found their own way of achieving this. This commonality of objective does sometimes lead to quite formulaic practice – after all, if you have a formula that works, why would you change it? Good results are not a bad thing of course, but they often drive focus towards the summative assessment and teaching strategies which lead to assessment success, or at the very least to providing evidence that the processes are working. It is a difficult balance – all teachers want their students to achieve, but most are also aware that education is about so much more than exam results and feeding the desires of the 'exam factory' (Coffield and Williamson, 2011). Doing the best for your learners sometimes means challenging the status quo – it requires the ability to not only think differently, but also to find your voice.

THE CHALLENGE OF TRYING TO THINK DIFFERENTLY

──────── CASE STUDY ────────

Eddie was a boy who had failed throughout his school years. He appeared a threat to his teachers. He would not conform. He seemed to have potential, but in his teachers' eyes he seemed to go out of his way to be "difficult". He was a born mismatcher. A misfit in the miseducation system.

He left school at 15 without grades or qualifications. He applied for a job in a government-run warehouse. And with it being a government-run warehouse, there had to be a government-approved interview, conducted by a government-approved interviewer. And the interviewer, like the teachers, expected the right answer to the government-approved questions.

"OK", said the interviewer, "first a general knowledge question. How many days of the week begin with the letter T?" Even the interviewer was surprised by the time it took Eddie to answer. Finally Eddie said, "Two."

"Correct," said the interviewer. "By the way, what are they?"

"Today and tomorrow," Eddie replied.

"OK," said the interviewer, thinking, 'I'll fix you wise guy'. "Here's a mathematics question. How many seconds are there in a year?"

Quick as a flash Eddie replied, "Twelve."

"Twelve," echoed the interviewer with incredulity. "How the heck did you get to that answer?"

"Well, that's easy," said Eddie. "There's January second, February second, March second, April ...."

"OK, OK. Here's a spelling question. How many Ds are there in Rudolph the Red Nosed Reindeer?"

Again there was a long silence. Eddie seemed engaged in some complicated internal-computation, nodding his head rhythmically. Finally, he said, "A hundred and three."

"A hundred and three? A hundred and three? Where do you get that answer from?"

"Da da da da da da dah. Dah da da da dah dah dah. Dah da ...."

(Grinder in Owen, 2001: 82-83)

As suggested by this story, thinking differently isn't always recognised by others as a good thing and yet, this ability is at the forefront of innovation. Formalised education (like many corporate organisations) is run within a certain framework which sometimes fails to value that which is different. You can see examples of this throughout history, particularly if you look at school experiences of some of the people now recognised as among the geniuses of the world. Leonardo da Vinci 'confounded' his schoolmaster with insistent questioning, Einstein was famously told he 'would never amount to anything' and Edison was considered awkward, his teacher apparently describing his brain as 'addled' (Gelb and Miller Caldicott, 2009). it is to be hoped that our understanding of both the human brain and behaviour has progressed since then and we have a much better understanding of the reasons behind difference as well as how to accommodate this within the classroom. Our own experience can certainly provide anecdotal evidence of teachers who strive not only to understand their learners but also to find creative ways of working with them as individuals. However, can the same be said for the ways in which teachers are accommodated? Is the teacher who thinks differently, who questions, who critically evaluates, supported in the same way as we might support our learners?

Figure 5.2   Flexibility

THE iMPORTANCE OF TAKiNG A FLEXiBLE APPROACH

It is easy to see how the way in which education has developed over the years has led to more structured forms of management and some of the reasons for this have been explored in previous chapters. The result is that we now work within quite stringent frameworks which do have a significant impact on our day to day activities. For most of us, the easy route is to conform to requirements and accept the system as it is; but, there will be times when suggested practice will not meet the needs of our learners and this is when we need to increase our ability to be flexible. In *Teaching as a Subversive Activity*, Postman and Weingartner (1971) question the overall role of the educator and conclude that our main objective should always be to provoke a spirit of enquiry in both ourselves and our students. This does bring to mind images of the campaigning teacher, firing up the enthusiasm of their students like Robin Williams in *Dead Poet's Society* or Michelle Pfeiffer in *Dangerous Minds*, but in practice this approach is likely to be tamed by the need to conform to some processes, such as following a scheme of work, syllabus or assessment plan. What it really means is that we need to be mindful of our values in relation to teaching and learning and develop the ability to be flexible in order to find a suitable route through and around the regulations.

REFLECTION

In Chapter 1 we asked you to reflect on your values in relation to your role. We now want you to consider some of the things within your teaching environment that challenge your values. Then consider how you might address these challenges by taking a more flexible approach. We are challenging you to find the 'VCF' (Value, Challenge, Flexibility), for example:

My value is that learning should be about discovery.

The challenge for me is that we are required to teach to the test

I could be more flexible by flipping learning. I could use a virtual learning environment to provide guidance required to support assessments and use class time for discovery activities.

THE iMPACT OF ROUTiNE

Routine is a natural part of life and, for most of us, daily routines fill our time in ways that we rarely question. We have a multitude of commitments and events which are woven into the fabric of our work so firmly they become embedded through habit. So much so that we often can't remember why we do things in that particular way and often, when challenged, it is not only difficult to envisage a different approach, it is quite likely that we might even be resistant to change. As highlighted in the previous activity, just taking a step back to remember our values, what challenges them and how we might address those challenges is a step towards a more flexible and authentic approach.

Whatever type of organisation you work in, the ability to be flexible can be a significant asset. Commercial businesses need to be aware of current market trends as well as have the ability to proactively create a new trend. In exactly the same way, the education sector must be aware of the needs of learners, employers and other stakeholders but must also have the ability to futureproof the curriculum – after all, schools, colleges and universities are preparing the leaders, scientists, entrepreneurs and creators of the future. This is not an occupation in which we can rely on being reactive – it is one which should be at the forefront of innovation and ensure that it is proactive in everything it does.

TRANSFORMATIVE LEARNING AND DISORIENTATING DILEMMAS

According to Mezirow (1991) there can be great value in the disruption of routines, particularly in the way we address particular events that cause us to reflect on our actions. Mezirow used the term 'disorientating dilemma' to describe those moments when previously accepted knowledge was challenged and as a result we may realise that we have been wrong about something. This might be a simple misunderstanding like not realising that 'lol' in text messaging means 'laugh out loud' rather than 'lots of love', or it could be something more significant such as changing a religious standpoint or being made redundant. Whatever the disorienting dilemma is, the realisation that your routine (or in some cases your basic assumptions) have been challenged can lead to anxiety, unease or even panic so it is not surprising that we generally avoid such change. However, in Mezirow's view this is not the approach to take if we want our learning to be transformative. By challenging our routines and our thinking, we have the opportunity to explore new knowledge which can be utilised in the future. This can open up new ways of looking at things which can alter our view of the world. Consider this from the point of view of your role as an educator – is this what you want to encourage in your students? If so, do the current structures in your organisation allow for this?

STRATEGIES TO INCREASE FLEXIBILITY

Developing a more flexible approach sounds like such a simple thing but it is important to remember that we are mostly creatures of habit and it is generally easier to do exactly what we have done before and, when things don't go according to plan, to blame events outside our control, or better still, just blame other people. That way we get to absolve ourselves of responsibility altogether! That might sound flippant but we suspect some of it will be familiar. It is probably true to say that most of us think we are flexible until it comes time for us to change. It is also true that if we continue to do things in the same way we will most likely get the same results. You may have heard the quote 'If you always do what you've always done, you'll always get what you've always got' (in Jeffers, 1988: 149). Perhaps more importantly we need to consider the development of our thinking in order to avoid stagnation, which means we should be willing to challenge ourselves, which as suggested by Blake means changing now only what we think but how we think: 'The man who never alters his opinion is like standing water and breeds reptiles of the mind' (Blake in Robbins, 2001: 277).

So ... how do we go about developing our flexibility? The first thing to remember is that like developing physical flexibility we need to stretch ourselves and acknowledge that it takes practice. You wouldn't expect to do a full yoga routine if you haven't exercised for years so it is probably wise not to expect a change in thinking or habits instantly.

RECOGNISING ROUTINES

One issue that we have not yet touched upon is the recognition of routines. By their very nature, routines are often difficult to identify as they are engrained into our day to day lives. We are often not aware of a particular routine until something happens to bring our attention to it. This may happen as the result of a disorientating dilemma (Mezirow, 1991) but it might also be useful to take a more structured approach. One effective way to do this is through reflection, which we will explore in more detail in Chapter 7. For now, the suggestion is simply to spend time thinking and writing about your routine activities and thoughts. There are several ways you can do this:

- Running commentary – a popular technique in advanced driving courses! If you keep a running commentary going in your head that tells you exactly what you see and how you react, it makes you think about any routines you have slipped into. Some people might want to actually say what you are doing, but doing it in your head works just as well.

- Diary writing – keeping a diary is a useful reflective tool at any time and it is particularly good when you are identifying patterns of behaviour. Remember to look back over your diary regularly and spot connections which might well indicate routines.

- A Friend Indeed – this is often the hardest technique to use but it does have the advantage of using the insight of someone who is removed from the process. If you get a friend to identify your routines then it is important to reassure them that this is being done to help you, otherwise they might be rather reticent about the process!

DEVELOPING SELF-EFFICACY

An important aspect of developing flexibility is building our sense of self-efficacy – the belief that we have the ability to influence events in our lives (Bandura, 2008). What we think, believe and feel are all parts of the self-system which in turn influences our actions. Self-efficacy not only shapes how we think and feel about things, it also has a significant impact on our ability to challenge current approaches. Someone with a strong sense of self-efficacy might display the following characteristics:

- Sees problems as challenges

- Develops an intrinsic interest in activities – wanting to know more

- Has a strong sense of commitment to their interests and activities

- Recovers quickly from setbacks and disappointments

- Is not put off by failure but sustains efforts towards achieving desired outcomes.

Figure 5.3 Self-efficacy

TAKiNG A KALEiDOSCOPE APPROACH TO THiNKiNG

Kaleidoscope thinking is based on Edison's strategy for innovation, which relies on viewing problems from every angle and making creative connections through a mental kaleidoscope by using both reasoning ability and imagination to liberate the mind from the constraints of habitual thinking. In essence this is about stretching our brains in the same way that we might stretch our muscles (Gelb and Miller Caldicott, 2007).

THiNKiNG iN SHADES OF GREY

This is really about avoiding all or nothing thinking. Most things have both positive and negative elements; thinking in shades of grey allows us to see this and provides a strategy for looking at situations more objectively.

ACTIVITY

As an example of what we mean by 'shades of grey' try to answer the following questions in just one word:

- Is stealing always wrong?
- Would you save one person from having a fatal accident if you know that three others will die if you take this course of action?
- Is there intelligent life anywhere else in the galaxy?

Whilst it is certainly possible to simplify your answers to a single word, clearly this is not something that we would be happy with; the nuances and complexity of the questions would be lost and strategising any plans based on this brief answer would be very difficult.

By thinking in shades of grey we can of course take a more balanced view of each of the questions in the activity and in doing so, provide a more reasoned response.

THINKING CRITICALLY

Familiar practice can so easily become a comfort blanket and leads to forms of automatic thinking. This is the sort of thinking that is essential in carrying out our day to day activities; it helps us juggle the demands on our time and tends to lead to automatic responses – which it could be argued may not be a product of thought at all! In order to challenge our practice we also need to challenge ourselves through critical thinking which, according to Brookfield (2012) has four key aspects:

- Hunting assumptions
- Checking assumptions
- Seeing things from different viewpoints
- Taking action.

DEVELOPING CURIOSITY

Being curious makes us much more open to new possibilities and provides us with tools to look at things from a range of perspectives. Developing curiosity requires having an open mind and accepting that what you 'know' might change. It also involves asking lots of questions to explore ideas. Being curious opens up our ability to be creative because there are always things to attract our attention or ideas to toy with. Curiosity is a natural state for some people, but even if it isn't there are ways of enhancing it.

- Avoid labelling things as boring or interesting – this limits focus. If something hasn't grabbed your attention yet it may need further exploration.

- Learn new things and have fun doing that. It is amazing how ideas can be transferred from one sphere to another, so don't be surprised if learning how to play a musical instrument leads you to ideas about new approaches to teaching.

- Make small changes to daily habits, change your routines in simple ways. This easy step provides you with a fresh outlook, even if it is just on one small part of your day.

Figure 5.4 Curiosity

THOSE WHO ARE FLEXIBLE HAVE THE MOST INFLUENCE

Behavioural flexibility is about modifying our own behaviour in order to get the outcome we want. It means adapting different approaches for different contexts. Flexibility is a fundamental aspect of change and has a number of benefits as it allows us to expand thinking and see a range of perspectives. It helps us to adapt to new circumstances, find solutions to problems and transform relationships. If we are flexible we have influence.

CHAPTER SUMMARY

In this chapter we have focused on achieving flexibility within the strictures of the current educational sector. This can be a challenge for two main reasons. Firstly, because the focus of the sector has been on improving standards by finding a formula that works for everyone. Whilst the aim is laudable, it does mean that individuality is not always encouraged and any teacher looking to work more flexibly might be viewed as 'challenging' the system.

The second problem is that routines come naturally to many people and there is a danger that this stifles any flexibility as teachers need to confront their own routines before changing their professional practice.

We will leave you with two questions to think about:

- To what extent are you bound by formulas for practice?

- What strategies could you adopt to increase your flexibility both in thinking and in practice?

FURTHER READING

Peters, S. (2012) *The Chimp Paradox: The Mind Management Programme to Help You Achieve Success, Confidence and Happiness*, London: Vermilion.

6

THE TEACHER YOU THINK YOU ARE IS THE ONE YOU WILL BE

In this chapter we will consider:

- The influence of thought and language on our experience
- The impact of expectations on events
- The power of learned optimism in developing agency

INTRODUCTION

In Chapter 2 we considered the ways in which our world view shapes the meaning we give to our work. It influences our perception of events, creates habits of thought and action, as well as providing the framework for how we perceive the role and our purpose within it. In a sense it defines our 'truth' about professional practice. Much of this is based on our training and the tacit knowledge developed through experience as well as any professional development we undertake; we not only gather skills and knowledge but also a range of attitudes and beliefs which certainly have an influence on what is 'true' for us. This is the essence of examining the teacher we think we are and the foundation of our professional identity. In this chapter we will explore the ways in which our thoughts influence our language and our practice and how our overall expectations of our role can have a significant impact on actions and outcomes.

REFLECTiON

Imagine that you are in an interview for a new job, the interview is going well and it is clear that the panel likes your approach. The final question is: 'what is your vision for this role?' How might you respond?

Would your response focus on the wording of the job description or the person specification? This might be a safe bet as it represents what the panel are currently looking for in a candidate. Or perhaps you would consider what you would like to see in the job? This is a more risky approach, but says something about your sense of vision as well as the agency you feel you would have in the role. There are a range of possible answers to this question of course, each saying something different about how you identify with your professional role.

Your answer will reflect many factors, but at the heart of it is the narrative that you build up around yourself and your job. *Narrative identity* refers to the ways in which we integrate our life experiences into an evolving life story. By combining our reconstructed past, our perceptions of the present and our imagined future, we create a sense of unity and purpose in life. In a sense it is a life story, with characters, a plot and episodes. What is significant about this, is that the way we construct our stories has an impact on how we live them. Research suggests that when our stories include themes of personal agency and exploration we tend to enjoy higher levels of mental health and well-being (Adler, 2012).

THE iNFLUENCE OF THOUGHT AND LANGUAGE

There is a well-known quote from Hamlet which expresses the importance of thought succinctly: 'There is nothing either good or bad, but thinking makes it so' (Hamlet, Act 2 Scene 2). The notion that thoughts are things (Mulford 2011) and can help manifest actual events is a popular one. That may be a matter of debate, but we know enough about the influence of our mindset to realise that thoughts most certainly impact on our actions and that we are both a product of them and a servant to their demands. At a fundamental level, thoughts are energy which direct the automatic functions of our body without, it seems, much thought at all! But they do take on form when emotions are attached to them and they can direct our personal and professional lives in significant ways. In a moment's thought we may commit to something that will move us in the direction of our goals or lead us up a completely different path. Similarly, some thoughts can fester, creating reality out of fantasy. There is certainly no denying the power of our thinking.

The language we choose can influence the image we project to others and how we talk about our professional role speaks not only of our perception of the role itself, but also of how we identify with it. Consider the difference between 'I am only a ...' and 'I have a really important role in ...'. Each conveys a very different picture. The stated role might well be the same, what differs is the narrative we have constructed around it and our words provide some insight into our sense of professional identity as well as the agency we feel within the role.

---- CASE STUDY ----

Rachel felt really lucky to have been offered a job at such a great college. She had no idea how she did, though - it must have been some sort of fluke. The team were great, the students were motivated ... what more could she want? The only problem was that the Head of Department wanted to observe her teaching tomorrow. She was beginning to panic; now she would be found out and they would realise that they had made a mistake.

Her thoughts were beginning to spiral as Rachel told herself that *she always* did badly when people watched her teaching, she would definitely lose the plot with the lesson and she knew that *the HoD would think* that she should never have been appointed. This was it, *she would be found out and would lose her job*. Even worse, if that happened she would be *completely lost and would never find another one*. She just knew she wasn't going to be able to sleep now.

Rachel had created a very definite thought pattern around her upcoming experience which had evolved into distinct forms of distorted thinking. She was making generalisations when she told herself that she *always* did badly when she was observed. This led to mind reading in assuming that she knew what the Head of Department would think and some fortune telling when she suggested that this would mean she would lose her job. Finally, she ended the thought process by catastrophising the whole event and told herself that she would lose the job and would never get another one. Needless to say that, especially after reinforcing the idea in her final thought, it was unlikely that she would get any sleep before the event and as a result would probably not perform as well as she could have done.

Distorted thinking is a common activity for many of us and can have a significant influence on our language and actions (Butler, Grey and Hope, 2018). Table 6.1 outlines some of the key forms of distorted thinking, including some of the things Rachel was telling herself about her upcoming observation.

Table 6.1   Types of distorted thinking

Type of distortion	Examples
Generalising - making assumptions based on something that has happened before. Often preceded by 'always', or 'never'.	'I always do badly when I am being observed.' 'Things never go right for me.'
Mind reading - we think we know what someone is thinking even though we have no evidence.	'The HoD will think I should never have been appointed.' 'They will think I am incompetent.'
Fortune telling - predicting an outcome without considering the facts.	'I will be found out and will lose my job.' 'This is bound to go wrong.'
Catastrophising - predicting the worst outcome and something will become a 'disaster'.	'I will be completely lost and will never find another job.' 'If this happens I will lose my mind.'

LiNGUiSTiC RELATiViSM

Linguistic relativism is based on the idea that language is a distinct human process which is connected to mental functions. It suggests that the language we use has an impact on cognition, particularly habitual patterns of thought (Batista, 2017); therefore, our perceptions are related to our language even when we are not aware of it. A pioneer in this area, Alfred Korzybski, showed how language influences our view of the world (Korzybski, 1958), an idea that led to the study of how semantic patterns influence cognition. If this is the case, then it follows that the manipulation of language may also be used to influence cognitive patterns and processes. This idea forms one of the key pillars of neuro-linguistic programming (NLP) – an approach to communication and personal development (Bandler and Grinder, 1975). The theory suggests that there is a connection between neurological processes, language and behavioural patterns and that by using a set of specific strategies behaviour can be changed in order to achieve specific goals. The 'touch of magic' offered by NLP has been popular, but it has also been discredited as a pseudoscience (Thyer and Pignotti, 2015). The core of this dispute seems to be around any scientific claims that are made, as the mixed bag of techniques, adapted from a range of disciplines, do not necessarily sit well with the scientific community. However, as Koestler suggests, 'Science is said to aim at Truth, Art at Beauty; but the criteria of Truth (such as verifiability and refutability) are not as clean and hard as we tend to believe, and the criteria of Beauty are, of course, even less so' (1964: 28).

NLP PRESUPPOSiTiONS

NLP is based on four key principles (referred to as 'pillars') – these are:

- Sensory acuity, which refers to increased awareness. It is about paying attention to what works and what doesn't, in order to match effort to desired outcomes.

- Behavioural flexibility is based on the idea that we have more influence if we have a range of responses to events and are not stuck in what we have always done.

- Rapport is linked to the development of harmonious relationships with others.

- Outcomes – ultimately NLP is goal-orientated. It is built on the premise that by changing the way we think and behave we can achieve the things we want to achieve.

In a pragmatic way, all of these things make absolute sense and many of the ideas have been explored already. In Chapter 2 we discussed the influence of world view, in Chapter 3 we explored the importance of compassionate communication and in Chapter 5 we explored the importance of behavioural flexibility.

When looking at thought, language and behaviour, the key element to consider is the idea of pre-suppositions. These represent basic assumptions we might make, which in turn influence what we believe and what we do. In our view, the presuppositions are designed to be powerful statements, which have the potential to influence reflection. We haven't included all of them in this chapter but have focused on the ones most related to teaching and learning. Their appeal is not universal – there are likely to be some that you really agree with and some that you don't and in the interests of respecting your choices, a good starting point is to test out your first reactions.

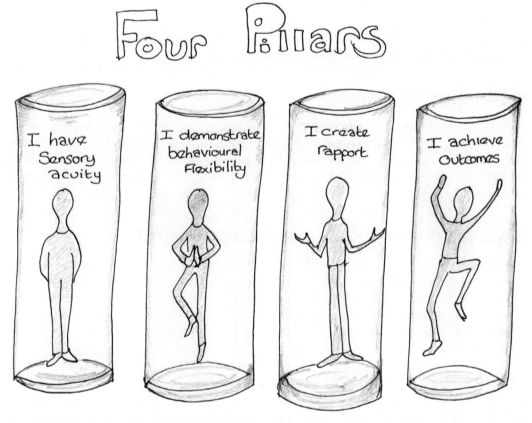

Figure 6.1   Four pillars of NLP

ACTIVITY

Read through the NLP suppositions in this list without making reference to the more detailed descriptions. At this point you are simply looking at the words and your own ideas about what they mean. Select the ones that you agree with, or perhaps would like to agree with. Then read the more detailed descriptions and reflect on whether or not these ideas already influence your practice or how you would like your practice to develop.

- 'The map is not the territory'
- 'The meaning of your communication is the response you get'
- 'A person is not his or her behaviour'
- 'Those with the most flexibility have the most influence'
- 'We are all parts of a system'
- 'We have all the resources we need to succeed or we can create them'

Your selection may already tell you about the things that are important to you and as a result the things which influence your practice. As you will have noticed, we have used some of the presuppositions to frame earlier chapters as these reflect our professional experience and have helped us to develop our understanding of teaching and learning processes.

THE MAP IS NOT THE TERRITORY

We have dedicated a whole chapter (Chapter 2) to this idea so probably don't need to say too much about it here. What is important about this is the recognition that our own world view isn't the only view and that our professional development is dependent upon our ability to think beyond what we already know and in doing so, making sure that we respect other people's maps or representations of the world.

THE MEANING OF YOUR COMMUNICATION IS THE RESPONSE YOU GET

It is easy for any of us to send out a different message to the one we intended and to resist messages we don't want to receive. Both of these things will impact on the effectiveness of a given communication. This, coupled with the idea that you cannot *not* communicate, illustrates the importance of thinking about how we communicate ourselves and how we interpret communication from others. The does stress the importance of communicating with clarity and compassion.

A PERSON IS NOT HIS OR HER BEHAVIOUR

All of the things we do are intended to achieve something, whether or not that is in our conscious awareness. As discussed in Chapter 4, all of our behaviour has a positive intent – even if that intent is to gain negative attention! This presupposition is about the importance of understanding behaviour and not simply making assumptions about it or categorising it as 'good' or 'bad'. When our intention is to reduce unwanted behaviour we can start this by finding the positive intent behind the behaviour and satisfying it in more appropriate ways. For example, a learner disrupting a lesson by playing the class clown has a reason for doing this, very probably that they simply want some attention which they could easily get by doing something else, such as by having some responsibility in the class or by helping other learners.

THOSE WITH THE MOST FLEXIBILITY HAVE THE MOST INFLUENCE

As outlined in Chapter 5, the more behavioural options we have available to us, the more flexibility we will have in how we respond to events. Things rarely go exactly to plan, so having more choices and being able to respond in a variety of ways does help us to achieve our outcomes – if something isn't working for us we will simply try something else.

WE ARE ALL PARTS OF A SYSTEM

Often this presupposition is focused on the links between body and mind and the influence one might have on another. In our view the idea is about much more than that and links back to feedback loops which occur in all aspects of life including nature, business and human relations (Bateson, 1970). When we interact with people, animals or objects we receive some feedback. A person's words or actions represent a form of feedback, a dog's friendly nudge or growl does the same and this feedback usually has the impact of moderating our own behaviour. When someone smiles at us we might start a conversation, if they look away we are unlikely to persist, if we receive a nudge from a friendly dog we are likely to respond with a stroke but might move away if we get a growl. Our actions in turn provide feedback to others involved in the interaction. A technical representation of this would simply be that outputs from a system are fed back as inputs, which in turn influence outputs.

If we view feedback loops as a cause and effect model, the idea seems simple; however, simple causal relationships are not that easy to pinpoint because all parts of the system are providing feedback which influences the overall interaction. So, A influences B, and the response from B influences A and so on. This stresses the importance of recognising the systems we work within and how they influence our practice. Practice cannot be changed in isolation – we must look at the system as a whole if we want to create a change which has impact.

Figure 6.2 disorientating dilemma

WE HAVE ALL THE RESOURCES WE NEED, OR WE CAN CREATE THEM

The idea behind this presupposition is that we are all resourceful and as a result can create the outcomes we want. Whilst there is some truth in this, it is also true that some people have more natural resources than others and this statement may be somewhat easier for them to put into practice. For us the key message is about developing autonomy. Whatever our starting point, we can all find strategies that will work for us but we need to take charge of a situation in order to do that.

DISORIENTATING DILEMMAS

In Chapter 5 we discussed the concept of transformative learning (Mezirow, 1991) and the impact of disorienting dilemmas which may shake up our current view of the world and at the same time present an opportunity to transform our practice. Imagine life to be a snowglobe, a safe, ordered world in which the landscape is clear; then, picture shaking it up, the 'snow' goes everywhere, it settles in a different place, landscapes that were previously clear have become obscured and new ones have emerged. When your beliefs are challenged, it can have a similar effect to the snowstorm and your world. In the workplace, these confusing shake-ups are a frequent occurrence and may make us question our previously held beliefs.

COGNITIVE DISSONANCE

When events challenge our belief structure, it can be a little disconcerting and very often has the impact of making us question what it is we actually know. You think you have a good understanding of something and then that understanding is challenged in such a stark way that it requires a complete rethink. Just think about how learning theories have changed over the years – in the Victorian era behaviourism was the order of the day and children were subjected to teaching and learning relationships based on positive and negative reinforcement (usually the latter); then we embraced a more humanistic approach and started to explore ways in which learning could become autonomous; then came evidence-based practice with its plethora of theories to incorporate – it is confusing to say the least. When our understanding is challenged it is unsettling. Festinger (1957) referred to this as cognitive dissonance, a term used to describe a feeling of extreme discomfort that we need to address if we want to restore a sense of balance. Let's look at a few examples to highlight what this means:

- You join a school that streams children according to their ability when you do not believe in this practice.

- Your college tells you to increase the marks of your students when you believe that they are currently a fair reflection of their ability.

- You are asked to do differentiated objectives for your sessions when you do not believe this is positive for your learners.

In each of these examples your values and beliefs might well run contrary to those that the organisation espouses; however, you are likely to have to follow the rules that are set down. This can cause feelings of discombobulation as you struggle to come to terms with what you are being asked to do.

Festinger suggests that we have an inner drive to keep our attitudes and beliefs in harmony so will adapt behaviours that enable us to do this; this means we could:

- change our beliefs to fit in with those being proposed – you may decide that actually there is some benefit to streaming children according to ability;

- acquire new information that helps reduce the dissonance – perhaps you find some research that advocates an uplift in marks in order to increase motivation;

- use internal reasoning and justification to accommodate the dissonance – you may tell yourself that differentiated objectives are a good idea after all; besides the managers love them so where's the harm?

THE iMPACT OF EXPECTATiONS

THE PYGMALiON EFFECT

The Pygmalion effect is a term linked to the research of Rosenthal and Jacobson (1968b) based on the idea that teachers' expectations can influence learners' behaviour and achievements. The main premise is that if teachers believe their learners are likely to succeed, they will treat them differently and in turn if learners realise that they are expected to succeed, they are more likely to meet expectations. There are similarities to Dweck's (2006) ideas about mindset, which linked achievement to whether or not learners had a growth mindset (and could apply themselves to address setbacks in learning), or a fixed mindset where they believed their basic intelligence and abilities were fixed traits – therefore whatever they did, it would not make any difference. Merton's ideas about 'self-fulfilling prophecy' encapsulate both of these theories (Merton, 1948). As the name suggests, this highlights the links between expectations and outcomes – simply put, a belief or expectation about what will happen for us, whether correct or incorrect, will come true because we will adapt our behaviours in order to fulfil that belief.

Rosenthal and Jacobson's original work looked at Mexican students (as well as other disadvantaged groups) who were participating in the US education system (Rosenthal and Jacobson 1968b). These groups historically underperformed compared to their peers and that was the narrative that was often carried into the classroom by their teachers who (either consciously or subconsciously) expected them to perform at a lower level than their peers. Although the original research focused on the attitudes of the teachers towards their classes, this could also apply in a wider sense when we consider accepted social norms. The idea that we are born into a set position in society is not a new one (Antonovsky, 1967) and despite protestations to the contrary, your life chances are still very much influenced by the 'accident of your birth'.

As an example of this, imagine the three different scenarios below and then think about how the context influences how each individual might view their life chances:

- Growing up in a prosperous suburb, both parents are teachers and the person achieved 'A' grades in all exams before going on to a prestigious university at the age of 18.

- Being born in an inner-city area noted for high levels of crime and habitual drug use, the person rarely attended school as their parents did not stress its importance and only came to education relatively late in life after attending an Access course at a local technical college.

- Moving relatively recently to the UK after training to be a teacher in another country.

In each case the starting point is predetermined so has a fixed beginning and the background described has a significant influence on any outcome. By recognising that this starting point has a 'normal' path attached to it, we can begin to make some decisions about whether or not that path is what we want. Although we can never have full control of the final outcome, greater levels of awareness help us to acknowledge and challenge the structural barriers that do exist (Rosenthal and Jacobson 1968b).

THE POWER OF LEARNED OPTIMISM IN DEVELOPING AGENCY

Figure 6.3 Glass half full/empty

We usually recognise optimistic or pessimistic tendencies in others by the person's general approach to life and the way they talk about things. It is often referred to as 'glass half full/empty'. To those with an optimistic outlook, pessimists might seem to have a downer on everything, whereas those with a more pessimistic outlook, might describe optimists as being unrealistic, even delusional. Why is this important? Do our personality traits simply match one or the other?

Seligman (2006) outlines the impact of our thoughts on our actions: 'Our thoughts are not merely reactions to events; they change what ensues' (2006: 5), suggesting that the habitual way we explain events, our 'explanatory style', is more than just words. Explanatory style is based on the same premise as linguistic relativism, which was discussed earlier in the chapter and contains three key elements:

- Permanence – people who have a tendency to give up easily explain bad events as if they are permanent; for example, 'I will never be good at …'. This is considered to be a pessimistic explanatory style. Alternatively, those who see bad things as less permanent are considered to have an optimistic explanatory style; for example, 'I didn't do well on that occasion …'. However, when it comes to events perceived as good, this is switched around, someone with a pessimistic style might dismiss a positive event as a one-off – 'It was a stroke of luck' whereas someone with an optimistic style might see these things as more permanent – 'I am lucky.'

- Pervasiveness describes whether an event is attributed to something specific or is considered universal: 'Some people can put their troubles neatly into a box and go about their lives even when one important aspect of it – their job, for example, or their love life – is suffering. Others bleed all over everything' (Seligman, 2006: 46). Making universal explanations for failure suggest that it would be easier to give up on a cause rather than pursue it. In contrast, an optimistic style would provide a more specific explanation, attributing a less than satisfactory outcome to something more specific.

- Personalisation – this refers to whether or not we blame ourselves when things don't go according to plan. People who blame themselves when something bad has happened may have low self-esteem as a consequence – they see this as being a fault in themselves. In contrast, people who blame external events do not experience such a negative impact on their self-esteem – they have externalised the event and don't see it as being a result of their actions.

Seligman further suggests that we can actually learn the skills of optimism by changing our explanatory style, which in turn will influence the choices we make as well as the actions we take. If we change how we use language, we can influence how we think. This is a powerful claim but perhaps it should come with a caveat – learned optimism is not a form of magical thinking, we still need to take responsibility and sometimes things are down to us and not the fault of external factors. 'Life inflicts the same setbacks and tragedies on the optimist as on the pessimist, but the optimist weathers them better … bounces back from defeat, and, with his life somewhat poorer, he picks up and starts again' (Ibid.: 207).

A NOTE ABOUT AGENCY

As suggested in Chapter 2, professional identity and agency are closely connected to each other and the narrative you form around your role (and yourself) will have some influence on how agentic you feel, i.e. how much you feel you control your life or your life controls you. Although there are numerous views on the topic of agency, we have already stated that our view is that whilst this is often situated in practice, it is personal to individuals and takes the form of personal autonomy, or more specifically, the belief that you have autonomy.

Professional agency is so important not only because it enables your creativity in the role but also because of the impact it has on motivation and well-being – but it isn't a given. Your agency may well have to be claimed and the skills associated with learned optimism may have a significant impact on this. In order to *become* the teacher you want to be, you need to make sure that you *think* you are the teacher you want to be. Before we summarise the key issues we have discussed, consider this quote from the book *The Little Prince* as it neatly encapsulates exactly what we mean when we say that you can control the narrative:

> All men have stars, but they are not the same things for different people. For some, who are travelers, the stars are guides. For others they are no more than little lights in the sky. For others, who are scholars, they are problems ... But all these stars are silent. You – You alone will have stars as no one else has them.

(De Saint-Exupéry, 2000)

CHAPTER SUMMARY

This chapter has explored the ways in which thought influences language and in turn how this impacts on becoming the teacher you want to be. Not only do our previous experiences influence our expectations but the ways that we talk about our role and ourselves also has an impact – so thought, language and expectations all lead to experiences. Remember that you are the one who interprets your 'stars', describes them to others and chooses whether or not to follow their guidance. With that in mind, we will leave you with a few things to consider:

- Do you have a strong image of the teacher you want to be?

- What thoughts will guide your future practice?

—— FURTHER READING ———————

De Saint-Exupéry, A. (2000) *The Little Prince*, London: Macmillan.

7

REFLECTING ON REFLECTION

In this chapter we will consider:

- The importance of reflection
- Some of the potential dangers in reflection
- How to use models of reflection
- How to use reflection to inform action

INTRODUCTION

According to the Greek philosopher Heraclitus, change is a constant in life; it is all around us, every day is a new experience, every sunrise and sunset slightly different and yet, life retains a sense of uniformity. Most of us inhabit a world of routines and fill our days in very similar ways. Our professional lives have regular scheduled events and similar activities to complete, so much so we can trundle through an academic year without noticing the time pass us by. Reflection allows us to learn from our experiences, to challenge our understandings and to make more informed choices. Acknowledging that we work within a changing landscape is a part of the process; no two events are exactly the same but some of the things leading to those events may be very similar and it is possible to extract learning from one to inform another. Most professionals do build reflection into their practice, but not all actually use these reflections to change what they do.

We have already discussed a variety of topics which impact on our practice including: world view, disorientating dilemmas, the impact of thought on language and the need for flexibility. All of this is useful learning that may have a positive influence on our professional roles and there is one thing that all of these topics have in common. To utilise any of this learning we must reflect on our practice and, in doing so, discover how new knowledge might inform it. In this chapter we will explore the importance of critical reflection and consider some practical approaches to embedding reflection into day to day practice.

THE iMPORTANCE OF REFLECTiON

Critical reflection is a way of helping us to challenge and develop ourselves, as it causes us to unpick how and why we see and do things. This doesn't necessarily mean that we must constantly make changes, it simply means that we need to examine our practice in order to develop a thorough understanding of it and, in doing so, we may locate areas of it we want to change. Teachers very often have mixed views about reflective practice and there are many reasons for this. For example, being 'forced' to keep a journal during training may have become a time consuming activity that didn't seem to offer immediate value, or perhaps you work in a context where it is necessary to write a formal evaluation after every lesson? If that is the case, it may seem unnecessary to carry out further reflection. Sometimes these things can be viewed as additional burdens and it can be difficult to see any real benefit other than providing evidence for others. When reflection is an imposed duty and is done for the benefit of evidencing good practice, it loses its value. Reflection should be for you, it should be about deepening your understanding, enhancing your learning and providing inspiration for your practice.

ACTiViTY

Based on the premise that reflection is a tool you can use for your personal and professional development - try listing the reasons why it might be beneficial to you.

As outlined in Chapter 1, reflection has an important role in challenging hegemony, in particular those elements of practice so embedded that they have become sacrosanct. It also forces us to continue thinking about what we do and to continue exploring alternatives, so in a sense it creates an impetus for learning. There are many reasons to reflect, not only on practice but on life. There are aspects of transferability in most experiences and by reflecting on these critically we have the option of altering our perceptions and our responses. So, here are our top 10 reasons for doing it:

- Reflection provides a safe place to critically analyse our professional practice.

- It helps us to establish our values and explore our professional identity.

- It allows us to view things from a range of perspectives.

- It helps us to identify what we do well and what we need to improve and highlights any new skills we might wish to develop.

- It helps us to consider our decision-making process and helps inform future decisions.

- It helps us to view things objectively, allowing us to manage difficult episodes in our professional life.

- It can be a strategy for challenging what we do and in turn helps us to identify alternative approaches.

- It puts us in the 'driving seat' and can increase professional agency.

- It has the potential to enhance our creativity.

- Sharing our reflections with others helps to develop more collegiate approaches.

SOME DANGERS OF REFLECTION

Figure 7.1   Comfort blanket

One of the joys of reflection is its therapeutic value. Keeping a journal can be a cathartic process for some people and allows us to explore our concerns in a safe space. However, it can also provide a 'comfort blanket', keeping us secure in ways of thinking, which reinforce current perceptions, so it is important that reflections remain critical. Critical reflection requires us to review a range of perspectives; it is human nature to surround ourselves with people who think in similar ways to ourselves and whilst that can be reassuring, the worry is that it produces an 'echo chamber' where our views are constantly reinforced rather than being challenged.

Figure 7.2   Echo chamber

As we explore thoughts and feelings when we reflect, the process has an emotional element. This in itself isn't a concern, emotions are after all a part of everyday life, but they can become harmful if allowed to turn into negative rumination or self-flagellation. As Brookfield says '[it] is like laying down charges of psychological dynamite. When these assumptions explode … the whole structure of our assumptive world crumbles' (Brookfield, 1990: 178).

REFLECTION AND INTROSPECTION

Reflection is a critical and objective process which quite naturally leads to the exploration of a range of ideas; however, introspection is much more personal. Here our focus is to look inwards, as the main aim is the development of self-awareness through analysis of thoughts and feelings. Through the process we may learn to think about things differently, which in turn can influence our assumptions, beliefs and practice. However, this isn't always the case and one danger to be aware of is that of *confirmation bias*, which refers to a tendency to interpret things in ways which confirm already held beliefs. This is a form of cognitive bias and happens when we focus on aspects of an event which reinforce what we currently 'know'. When this happens, we are drawn to what supports our existing understandings and may well ignore the things that don't.

In a similar way, when we have to make decisions we use a process that relies on heuristics; these can be characterised as mental shortcuts which are based on our assumptions and previous experiences. This is a highly efficient process that allows us to make decisions quickly, but because it relies on using known patterns of thinking and doing, there is the danger that we might miss the critical information which may lead to better decisions.

CASE STUDY

Patrick, a very confident new teacher, has just had his first formal lesson observation. The observer spent a lot of time going through the feedback with him and summarised this with the following key points:

- A well organised and clearly structured lesson.
- You demonstrated good knowledge of your subject.
- Class management was effective in that learners were kept on task throughout. This was mostly achieved through a teacher-led approach.
- There were occasions when learners wanted to ask questions but were moved on very quickly.
- There was no evidence of differentiation in activities.

When Patrick's mentor asked for his reflections on the observation, Patrick's response was: 'It was great, the feedback was that I was well organised and I managed the class well, - and kept them all on task!'

For Patrick, this feedback simply confirmed what he already knew – that he was a competent teacher. In order to confirm this particular bias, Patrick had been selective in terms of which parts of the feedback he paid attention to and he had simply adapted his understanding of the rest. This allowed him to maintain his current perception. This required making his own decisions about what the feedback actually meant, for example: *This was mostly achieved through a teacher-led approach.* May have been interpreted as: *You led the class well*, and *There were occasions when learners wanted to ask questions but were moved on very quickly*, could have been understood as: *You made the best use of time*. If Patrick had been critically reflecting on this event, he would have asked questions and started a discussion about alternative approaches rather than choosing to interpret the feedback in a way that suited his current beliefs.

It is also possible for introspection to cloud our self-perception, particularly if we are searching for answers, sometimes resulting in a vicious cycle of negative thinking.

CASE STUDY

Bethan was looking for a promotion to a more senior role in her organisation and had been offered an interview for a new post. She was both excited and apprehensive about this, it was a great opportunity, but she suspected she had only been offered an interview because she already worked for the organisation. For days before the event she speculated about the questions, the priorities of the interview panel, how she might come across. She kept telling herself that she always got tongue-tied when she was nervous and she would undoubtedly be nervous. She also knew that she lacked some of the essential skills required for the job - what if she couldn't do it?

(Continued)

(Continued)

She definitely wasn't experienced enough and that panel would know that. She concluded that she probably didn't have a chance. When the interview came around, Bethan was honest with the panel and decided to address any concerns from the outset. She started by outlining her lack of experience and continued to point out all of the things she had been ruminating on over in the last few days.

The type of introspection which leads to excessive rumination can be just as dangerous as that which confirms our biases. It can cloud our perceptions, leading to negative consequences. In Bethan's case it probably led to her not being offered a job she may well have been very capable of doing.

Figure 7.3 Negative rumination

Having a greater understanding of ourselves is certainly helpful and is believed to support our relationships and well-being. Those with high insight are likely to feel more in control of life and have more personal growth (Harrington and Loffredo, 2010). However, the act of thinking about ourselves isn't the same as knowing ourselves, so we could spend hours on introspective naval gazing and have no more insight than when we started (Grant, Franklin and Langford, 2002). This is most certainly a danger of reflection and illustrates the importance of taking an objective and critical approach and where necessary, linking reflection to action.

THE NEED FOR A CRITICAL APPROACH

As we have suggested, reflection can very easily become a comfort blanket that we use to protect ourselves against things we don't want to think about. At the same time, it can also become an unhelpful form of self-flagellation, so it is important to develop an approach that enhances objectivity and criticality and one which helps widen our overall perspectives.

Habits of thinking are often based on assumptions that we have accepted as being accurate, whether they are actually accurate or not. Brookfield (2012) suggests that to improve criticality, there are four things to consider:

- Hunting assumptions

- Checking assumptions

- Seeing things from different viewpoints

- Taking action.

In addition, Table 7.1 outlines different types of assumptions: paradigmatic, prescriptive and causal:

Table 7.1   Different types of assumptions

Description	Example of assumption and challenge
Paradigmatic assumptions	
Internalised beliefs - these are the things we know to be true. They help structure understanding of the world and our purpose within it.	'Education is a social and democratic process.' The high cost of university fees may make education less democratic than we think.
Prescriptive assumptions	
What we think should be happening in a particular situation, for example the way someone should behave, things they should do or not do.	'University students should develop a deep interest in their chosen subject.' Education in the UK focuses primarily on summative assessment rather than deep learning.
Causal assumptions	
This is based on cause and effect relationships and relate to ideas about how one part of a system should react, following a specific action, for example if I do A then B will happen.	'Teaching and learning should be active and fun.' When learners are subjected to activity after activity with no chance to reflect on their learning or clarify understanding, this might be challenged.

Raising awareness of assumptions is only the first step. Once assumptions have been highlighted it is important to check their validity, which we can do by looking at them from a range of perspectives and considering alternatives, for example:

- What assumption am I making?

- What else could I assume?

- What might ... say about this assumption?

- When might this assumption be true or not true?

Perspectives may also be widened by looking at an event through different critical lenses, for example:

- Autobiographical lens – self-reflection relating to our personal experience both as teacher and learner.

- Students' views – looking at an event through the eyes of the students.

- Colleagues' views – considering what colleagues might say about an event or how they might have handled it.

- Theoretical lens – considering what the literature has to say, how might general theory apply to practice?

The lenses model (Brookfield, 2017) is useful as a tool to force us to think about how others might view a given situation and, whilst that seems obvious, it is surprising how often we see things in ways that are very familiar.

HOW TO USE MODELS OF REFLECTION

Models of reflection offer a framework for thinking critically. In our experiences there is no one 'best' model, each has its own strengths and weaknesses and you may find that different models are appropriate at different times. Table 7.2 outlines some of the most popular ones and provides suggestions for practical use.

Table 7.2   Using models of reflection

Model	Summary	Example of its practical use
Atkins and Murphy Cycle	The cycle is designed to get the user to think about a problem and to avoid superficial responses to events. A key stage is the analysis of feelings as well as knowledge.	Reflecting weekly on a particularly challenging class where you are keen to try new strategies each time you teach them.
Gibbs Reflective Cycle	A cyclical approach that takes a linear approach to reflection with users going through 6 stages.	You teach the same subject several times a week to different classes and want to learn from the experience.

Model	Summary	Example of its practical use
John's (2000) Model of Structured Reflection	A model that includes aesthetics (the art of what we do) and also ethics in amongst the stages.	You wish to increase the mark of a student who has worked very hard on their assessment but you are not sure whether this fits into the regulations.
Kolb's Experiential Learning Cycle (1984)	A classic model of reflection that asks the user to go through the following stages: Concrete experience (what happened) Reflection observations (reflections on events) Abstract conceptualisation (what does it mean?) Active experimentation (what else could I do?)	You are mentoring a particularly tricky mentee and want them to get into the habit of reflecting on their teaching rather than repeating the same mistakes.
Through the Looking Glass	This focuses on reflexivity and is based on 3 foundations: Certain uncertainty Serious playfulness Unquestioning questioning.	You team teach with another member of staff and after each lesson you relive the lesson together to see what you have learnt.
Schön Reflection in action – Reflection on action	This model is split into two parts – reflection in action – which is what happens during an event and reflection after the event – reflection on action.	The start of your lessons tends to be well controlled but you find yourself losing the class the further the session goes on. You may consider this reflection 'in-action' and 'on-action'.

Reflection can be any activity that prompts thinking about our experiences. We don't necessarily need a model to do this, but it may be a good starting point and information on all of the above models is readily available – we have included some links in the further reading section. In addition, it may also be useful to employ a range of short, reflective activities. The key is to start the process so that it becomes a regular part of what you do.

HOW TO USE REFLECTION TO INFORM ACTION

Systems theory sets out to develop an understanding of how things interact and is based on the premise that we are all parts of a bigger system that is closely linked via a range of cause and effect relationships. We introduced this idea in Chapter 6 when we considered the notion of feedback loops and the ways in which one part of a system influences the way other parts interact. According to Bateson, an important aspect of this is to discover the pattern that connects by exploring how different elements communicate. When we reflect what we are seeking is the key information which may change a perception or offer an important insight: 'a difference that makes a difference' (Bateson, 1972: 315). This can be applied to challenging situations by exploring the interaction-patterns which influence them and by locating patterns – things that repeat in a predictable manner. In doing so we may be in a position to influence positive change. This sounds like, and is, a very powerful idea but it comes with a caveat. In order to find the information that is likely to make a difference we may have to challenge assumptions and suspend current beliefs.

We may also need to try a range of strategies for reflection to ensure that we gain a variety of perspectives. A key issue in reflective practice is the way in which humans tend to 'story' information. We rarely store objective facts; it could even be argued that it isn't possible to even perceive things objectively, and when we convey information to others we tend to do so in the form of a story in which we have placed ourselves as a key character. In doing this we share events, perceptions, judgements – and maybe a little bit of creativity. We could even argue that our life is one long story, metaphor plays an important part in how we make sense of things and how we construct our stories is key to our interpretation of them.

The case studies shared earlier in the chapter provide examples of how this can play out in practice. Patrick's story is one of success. He clearly sees himself as a competent professional and seeks out patterns which reinforce this view. What he heard from the feedback he was given reinforced his current view. In Bethan's case the same was true but a completely different story; here we have someone who had already decided on the outcome of a particular event and structured her actions around the conclusion she had already adopted.

LiFE SCRiPTS

Transactional Analysis (TA) theory suggests that we have all constructed stories about our lives, referred to as 'life scripts' and similar to other therapeutic disciplines it is suggested that such scripts, which are constructed in childhood, develop into unconscious life plans that, without awareness, we live out faithfully. We create the script in childhood, partly linked to environmental factors but involving choice as the infant finds a strategy for survival (Stewart and Joines, 2012). The script is reinforced by parents through the messages they give to the child, the 'don'ts or shoulds'. By adulthood the script is outside of our awareness and the nearest we come to it is in dreams and fantasies and unless we take the time to explore these ideas we are likely to remain unaware of the full script. What we are more likely to do is to unknowingly influence our interpretation of events so that they match our script:

> *What we often do is to interpret reality in our own frame of reference so that it appears to us to justify our script decisions. We do this because, in our child ego state, we may perceive any threat to our script-based view of the world as a threat to the satisfaction of our needs or even a threat to our survival.*

> (Stewart and Joines, 2012: 101)

--- **REFLECTION** ---

Once upon a time

Booker (2005), in analysing the structure of stories, suggests there are key patterns amongst them and that there are only seven types of plot. These are:

1. Overcoming the Monster - the lead seeks out and, against all odds, destroys the monster so that safety may be restored.

2. Rags to Riches - a young hero/heroine is living a difficult or ordinary life. One day an event sends them out into the world and a magical transformation takes place.

3. The Quest - a call to action which involves a journey and a specific task.

4. Voyage and Return - The main character travels out of their familiar life to explore another world and are transformed in some way.

5. Comedy - confusion and uncertainty escalating into a tangle. Finally, this leads to a change in perception in which everything is resolved and ends happily.

6. Tragedy - in this story we still have our hero or heroine who form part of a community through friendship, family or love, they get caught up in a course of action with only one possible outcome.

7. Rebirth - the protagonist becomes overshadowed by a dark power which may grow and wane but eventually reveals its full force. They are able to change and be reborn.

Take a look at the seven basic plots and select the one you are most drawn to. Then, using the basic tenets of the plot, construct a personal story. What patterns do you recognise? What does this tell you about how you are constructing your own story?

Although Booker's work was originally based on creative storytelling, there are many links to how we might view our own lives. After all, what is storytelling if not a reflection of life? Recognising patterns is a way of uncovering elements of our story, or script; at the very least it highlights habitual behaviours which can be viewed objectively.

STRATEGIES FOR RECOGNISING PATTERNS

We all recognise that there is an element of routine in our working lives and most people would readily admit that some parts of their practice are steeped in habit. Some of these practices and habitual behaviours may have served us well and are things we want to maintain, but for those that don't it is important to highlight the patterns so that we may implement effective strategies for change. The following strategies offer simple ways of locating patterns and are things which can easily be built into reflective practice:

- Take 5 steps – this involves outlining a problem or concern that you have been thinking about (step 1); then list as many aspects of it as you can – anything that you have information about. What happened? The sequence of events? The apparent impact and so on (step 2)? Go back over the list and highlight any connections between the various parts (step 3); look for common themes or repeating patterns (step 4); rewrite the event (step 5).

- Write a line a day – line a day diaries allow you to log the events of a particular date and normally last for five years. The effect is that you can see exactly what happened on that day in previous years. They are quite a scary reminder of how predictable life can be!

- Ask the family (or friends) – given that it is often very difficult to identify our own patterns, one strategy we could use is to seek help from others. Asking family members or friends to identify your patterns or habits can be a bracing experience but it is a great way of identifying your patterns.

- Mr and Mrs – this is a similar technique to the previous one but relies on just one person who is very close to you. Write down a list of questions about yourself and then write down the answers (examples might be 'what dish would I choose in a Chinese restaurant?' 'What would I do if my best friend was in trouble?'). Next pass the questions on to the other person and see if they get the same answers – the similarities and differences can be illuminating.

- 5 minute download – this strategy is based on the idea that thought and language are closely connected and involves analysing the words we use. It involves spending five minutes writing down thoughts on the day. No editing should take place and writing should continue until the time is up. After several entries, the text is reviewed and any patterns indicated by repeated words or phrases are highlighted.

- Assumptions inventory – this is simply a way of recording key assumptions and can be added into any reflective journal. When recording your thoughts about a given situation, consider what your underlying assumptions are. This could be done simply by asking 'what assumptions am I making here?' which can then be challenged with 'what else could I assume?'. Assumptions which appear regularly and in different scenarios are an indicator of patterns of thinking.

- Video replay – this requires creating a relaxed state so is best preceded by some breathing exercises. Once relaxed, run the events of a particular incident through your mind as if watching a video replay of them, noting any tensions or positive feelings. This works well when you do it with a peer so that there is an opportunity to discuss the most memorable aspects.

- Storyboarding – a similar activity to the video replay in that you are mapping out a particular event through the use of a storyboard. The images don't need to be perfect – just representations of the key points.

All of the suggestions here are simply extensions of reflective practice and what works will differ from person to person. All forms of reflection will present the opportunity to locate patterns of thinking and behaviour; we simply need to take the time to utilise the often insightful information this presents. Once patterns have been detected, the next logical step is to consider what changes we might want to make and then set up a framework that supports the implementation of those changes. This will be covered in a little more detail in chapter 9.

Figure 7.4   Storyboard

CHAPTER SUMMARY

This chapter has considered the importance of reflection on our practice. The idea of reflecting on what we do isn't new but its importance in locating patterns of thought and behaviour that influence everyday activities isn't always recognised. We often reflect and then continue to do what we have always done. Reflecting on reflection is about using the activity to make positive changes and with that in mind, give some thought to the following questions:

- How might you uncover the assumptions which underpin your practice?

- In what ways can you utilise reflection to locate positive and negative patterns of thought and behaviour?

FURTHER READING

Bolton, G. (2014). *Reflective Practice: Writing and Professional Development* (4th ed.), Los Angeles, CA: Sage.

Brookfield, S. (1990) *Becoming a Critically Reflective Teacher*, San-Francisco: Jossey-Bass.

Thompson, C. (2021) *Reflective Practice for Professional Development*, Oxon: Routledge.

8

MANAGING THE ROLES WE PLAY

In this chapter we will explore:

- The roles we play in personal and professional life
- The importance of developing an authentic sense of self
- Appropriate impression management

INTRODUCTION

'Hello, may I introduce …?' Words that we hear many times a year, often accompanied by a handshake, and perhaps a few words of introduction, provide an opportunity to take in the other person. In those first few seconds we are likely to come to some initial conclusions about the person. These conclusions are drawn from scant evidence: how someone looks, the gestures they use, how they dress and perhaps how they speak. In an instant we have made a judgement that has no doubt categorised that person and informed whether or not we want to get to know them more. In more formal situations we may decide whether or not we want to offer someone a job or a new opportunity. The impression we have gleaned, whether genuine or not, has already had an influence. In this chapter we will explore the ways in which our interactions are influenced by the roles we play and how this informs the impressions others have of us. We will also consider the importance of authenticity in human relationships.

THE ROLES WE PLAY

Life's a stage! Goffman's dramaturgical theory is based on the idea that life is a never-ending play in which we are all actors (Goffman, 1959). From an early age, we are thrust onto the stage of life acting out the many roles we must undertake in the family, with friends, at work and so on. Each of these roles has expectations attached to it and we are likely to act in ways which meet those expectations; in this way we manage the impression others have of us but in turn are influenced by how others respond to us within these roles.

REFLECTION

Imagine yourself in each of the following scenarios. Think how you would dress, how you would talk, what language you would use, how you would address people; in fact think about the entire interaction that would occur:

- Your first class with a new tutor group
- Meeting your closest friends for a pub meal on a Friday night
- Attending a job interview for a role that you really want

The chances are that responses in each of these scenarios is likely to be quite different. There are lots of reasons for this, sometimes societal expectations affect how we portray ourselves (for example the necessity to be smart for a job interview), other times it is the presence of other people – you are likely to talk in a different way to friends than you would to your colleagues, but mostly it is down to the impression you portray to others as a result of the role you play in their lives. Goffman suggests that actors are constantly occupied with *impression management*, in influencing the impression that others have of them. In such cases the behaviour presented will be the behaviour that is likely to be that which is considered acceptable in a certain situation.

Goffman described the self as being constructed of both 'front stage' and 'back stage' elements. The front stage relates to aspects of self we present to the world, often a particular identity for a particular audience. It is here where we will try to manage others' impressions of us. Back stage personas represent who we really are. It is the back stage where we are likely to feel accepted and not have the pressure of trying to fit in with others' expectations – this could be considered our 'true self'.

REFLECTION

Think about your own front stage and back stage personas … is there ever a time when these might be in conflict? If so, what are the underlying reasons for the conflict?

The construction of the self is of course made up of a number of things such as world view, culture and the people we interact with, and whilst many of these things are firmly embedded they are not fixed constructs. As Bauman suggests, social construction is a changing landscape, so establishing a durable identity over an extended period of time is problematic; instead, the way we interact may be represented by the term 'liquid modernity' (Bauman, 2000). We need to adapt to changes in society and as a result may adapt our professional identities, particularly in a volatile sector such as education – often seen as the panacea to society's ills and as a result subject to regular change. As we write this we are experiencing the Covid-19 pandemic, a situation which has most certainly had an impact not only on how we view society but also on how we work within it. Many professions have been impacted by this and have had to find new ways of working, and many teachers are quickly developing a whole range of new skills they never expected to learn.

CASE STUDY

Lila had always been confident about her ability as a teacher. Partly that confidence came from feedback from her many teaching observations and partly from an inner confidence that was fed by her family's view that she was very talented at everything she turned her hand to - something they related to her on numerous occasions. She knew that others expected her to do well in the role and she did everything she could to meet these expectations, but the events of the last few days had started to shake her confidence.

Lila had been teaching her students online and was beginning to think she was failing them. She realised that her digital skills were not as good as those of some of her fellow tutors and she often made mistakes. She found herself talking to her classes whilst on mute, sharing the wrong screen, and even found her cloud account was not configured correctly, so her students grew frustrated when they couldn't access her resources.

As another class filled with technology glitches came to a close, Lila slowly closed her laptop and wondered where her previous confidence had gone to. She had failed to meet her own high standards and was beginning to question whether she really was a good teacher. She had even begun to think that maybe this wasn't the right job for her.

A change in self-perception can occur for any number of reasons and is not necessarily always negative; for example, a promotion or some good feedback might have a more positive impact. However, in Lila's case this had affected her at a deep level and she had begun to question her overall identity as a teacher. When we experience these things they can have a significant influence on how we feel about ourselves. Whether a change is positive or negative, it is accommodated into our sense of self and in turn on how others see us (Merrill, 2009).

IMPRESSION MANAGEMENT

Our front stage persona is something we have awareness of; indeed, it is something we deliberately create. For teachers there are certain expectations within the role, such as modelling professional behaviour, treating people with respect, dressing appropriately and so on. This understanding shapes how we might behave, which in turn shapes how others view us. These things don't necessarily play out on the back stage, where we might cast off the apparatus of our performance by swapping work clothes for something more casual; we may even speak and act differently. Whilst we may use 'back stage' to prepare for our front stage performance by rehearsing things such as a presentation, or an important conversation, we generally don't carry back stage behaviours into the public arena. Our public-facing self is much more likely to be tamed by our understanding of what others expect of us.

Figure 8.1   Impression management

Impression management is sometimes referred to as 'self-presentation' as it involves the processes undertaken to control how others perceive us. Most people are motivated to manage their public images as they see these as being inherently linked to their overall goals. Quite standard advice is 'dress for the job you want, not the job you have' which suggests that if we want to create the right impression then we need to plan ahead. This is not just about clothes of course but about personal presentation overall; how we act around others, how we interact in meetings; how we work with colleagues, respond to managers and so on. The term 'personal presentation' is often viewed as being more positive; unlike 'impression management' which can be viewed as potentially manipulative. When we consider personal presentation we might ask ourselves if we are simply being professional – or if we are being led by others' expectations.

DEVELOPING A SENSE OF SELF

The self might be defined as a person's essential being, their individuality, the aspects that distinguish them from others. The self is often something considered in introspection, whereby we may try to explore the consciousness of our being. For most people describing the 'self' as a concept

Answer the following two questions:

1. How would you define 'the self'?

2. Imagine you are on a first date and have decided to avoid all mating games in the interests of complete honesty and self-disclosure. How would you describe yourself?

would involve making reference to things such as self-identity or perhaps Ego. In Freud's view the self would consist of three parts, Ego, Super-ego and Id, each of which is located in different parts of the mind; for example:

Figure 8.2   Iceberg model

The Ego – the part of the mind focused on reason and logic which is located in the conscious mind. In the model, this is the tip of the iceberg. It deals with our automatic thinking or our day-to-day chatter.

 The Superego – the voice that incorporates values and morals, the things we have learned which make up our view of the world. Not always apparent at a conscious level, it traverses both the conscious and pre-conscious mind and its role is to keep the Id in check.

 The Id – this part of the mind is considered to be about natural instincts, physiological drives and impulses. Located in the unconscious mind, which is represented by the large mass hidden beneath the water line. Things hidden from consciousness but which still influence thoughts, behaviours and actions; apparently innocent unless hit by a passing ship!

Descartes takes a more dualistic view and suggests that the true self is something quite separate from the material body. Humans have both a mind, which is non-physical and a body/brain, which is made up of physical matter. The mind simply inhabits the body but is not a physical part of it; however, it does influence the body and vice versa. Whilst the mind may control actions, the body can also have an influence, for example when someone is driven by passion they may take over a normally rational mind (Cockburn, 2001; McCleod, 2018).

How did you define the self? And, how different was your definition of *the self*, from your description of *yourself*? What is interesting is that most of us would say that we have a 'self' but when describing ourselves to others, we are likely to outline the things on which judgements can be made; for example, we may say what job we do, or where we live, we may talk about our achievements or perhaps our hobbies. All of these things will paint a picture, perhaps of an image we want to portray, or, as in the case of the activity, of the way we view our life. This allows others to make a judgement about us in relation to their own lives and to decide if we are a good fit, someone they might like, want to befriend or want to start a relationship with.

Our sense of self is something which develops over time, we grow into it and we have usually fought a few battles to define it. When we have a strong sense of self, it is presented as who we are and as such is not something we will let go of easily. We will defend it as an important part of us and will also use it to compare ourselves to others, sometimes favourably, sometimes not.

ACTIVITY

Take a look at the following list and reflect on any times when you have felt one or more of these things.

- Inferior because colleagues seem to be more successful.
- Fed up that friends seem to be more popular or attractive.
- Somehow defective because you have a hidden flaw.
- Awkward when in social situations for fear of being judged.
- Afraid of speaking to large groups or presenting to colleagues because you might make a fool of yourself.

You may have felt all of these things at some point or another and can perhaps add one or two others. We are all quite good at viewing our limitations and often very good at beating ourselves up about them. However, some people do have the ability to view shortcomings as opportunities to learn new things or for personal growth, and there are a number of strategies that can be employed to do this. One of the first, and perhaps the most important is: 'What the Buddhists call the "Great Death" – allowing your self to die. You can suddenly experience profound growth, freedom and joy' (Burns, 2020: 364).

Having a strong sense of self can be helpful in forming values and in making choices. It provides the basis to live authentically but should also be brought into question when required.

THE AUTHENTIC SELF

We live in a society that is built on stories of success that are artfully managed through social media. At times it can seem as though everyone is not only more successful than us, they are also much more popular and have seemingly perfect lives. In this climate, owning your least successful moments can be a challenge and it is easy to see why there are some aspects or our self that we don't accept as readily as others. However, the practice of acceptance is seen as the first step to transformation, as this not only enhances self-awareness, but it also helps to break down the barriers to change. As Rogers stated: 'I find I am more effective when I can listen acceptantly to myself, and can be myself ... the curious paradox is that when I accept myself just as I am, then I change' (Rogers, 1961: 17). According to Brown, the journey to self-acceptance starts with being present and open to vulnerability: 'it's having the courage to show up and be seen when we have no control over the outcome' (Brown, 2012).

THE FULLY FUNCTIONING PERSON

The Rogerian approach is based on the idea that everyone can achieve their goals if the conditions are right and it identifies several characteristics of the fully functioning person (Rogers, 1961).

- Being open to experience and accepting of any emotions associated with our experiences.

- Living existentially – trying to live fully in the moment and avoiding always looking back or towards the future.

- Trusting feelings – paying attention to gut reactions, emotions and instincts. This requires having trust in ourselves to make the right choices. Belief in determining own behaviour, so responsible for own behaviour and choices.

- Creativity – thinking creatively and taking risks – not always feeling the need to play safe, which may mean developing the ability to adjust and to seek new experiences.

- A rich, full life – experiences joy and pain, fear and courage, love and heartbreak intensely. Requiring the courage to 'be'.

In the humanistic approach advocated by Rogers, all of this should be developed within a framework of unconditional positive regard, based on the belief that people are inherently good and seek personal growth. Developing unconditional positive regard is dependent on acceptance and support and creating a safe place which is free of judgement.

CASE STUDY

Kalvir recognised the importance of creating a nurturing environment within her classroom and felt that it was really important to generate a culture of respect in which every single person could recognise their value within the group. To do this she emphasised the importance of mutual respect and of embracing the learning experience and encouraged the asking of questions and sharing thoughts and opinions. She regularly reminded the learners that the group was a safe place and that thinking creatively was more important than getting the right answers, so they were safe to take risks with learning and try new things. This was something she genuinely believed and it paid off. Her groups were usually well-motivated, focused and coped with just about anything she threw at them. To teach them was an absolute joy.

Despite her success in the classroom, Kalvir was beginning to question her own judgement and was getting increasingly concerned about her teaching because she knew her approach was very different to her colleagues. Also, her Head of Department had told her that she needed to focus more on preparing the learners for assessments and shouldn't be wasting precious time in getting them to 'feel good about themselves'.

POSITIVE SELF-REGARD AND SELF-WORTH

Rogers believed that self-worth is something which could be viewed on a continuum and those with low self-worth were likely to lack the confidence to face challenges, whereas those with high self-worth would do so with confidence and would have the ability to view themselves positively even if challenges were not met (Rogers, 1959). In a nutshell – how we think about ourselves impacts on our achievements. More recent literature reinforces this idea. Bandura acknowledged the impact of self-efficacy on achieving outcomes (Bandura, 1986) and Dweck (2017) made reference to the impact of whether or not we have a growth or fixed mindset and how this would influence our approach to challenges. This theory suggests that those with a fixed mindset would see themselves as having fixed abilities and those with a growth mindset would see themselves as having untapped potential (Dweck, 2017). Similarly, Duckworth (2017) believes that to be successful we need to develop passion and resilience, we need to demonstrate 'Grit'. Whether we view this as self-regard, efficacy, mindset, grit or something else, there is evidence to suggest that the way we think about ourselves has a significant impact on what we can achieve. In Kalvir's case it was clear that she recognised the importance of developing a strong and positive sense of self and she had demonstrated that she knew how to do this. Unfortunately, she didn't seem able to extend this gift to a very important part of the group ... herself! As a result, she was very influenced by those around her; she didn't want to be too different from her colleagues despite the success she was experiencing in the classroom and she had been made very aware of her manager's expectations of her. This may lead to Kalvir changing her approach in order to fit in and meet others' expectations of her, even though what she was doing was clearly working.

Kalvir's story is one based on fear of the impression she was creating. She didn't want to give her manager the idea that she wasn't concerned about assessments but she also feared being seen as different to her colleagues. These fears were making her question her own judgement and potentially inhibiting her development. When you work in an environment where job security is a fluid concept (as is the case in some areas of the education sector), the need to fit in can be even more apparent: '[fear] makes us want to retreat into our shells and reach for safety. Although that is tempting, it stops us changing, it gets in the way of solving problems and resolving our difficulties' (Butler, Grey and Hope, 2018: 399).

One way of overcoming this is to develop a deeper sense of curiosity, to explore our fears and test their validity; in this way we may discover the real extent of perceived fears and sometimes we can see that the biggest fear is the fear itself – the thought rather than any tangible danger.

ACTIVITY

Thought experiment

A thought experiment is a way of mentally testing something out. Start with bringing a particular difficulty to mind. Then work through the following steps:

- Identify your safety behaviours - the ways in which you protect yourself in relation to this difficulty (for example, hiding away from it or pretending the problem doesn't exist).
- Ask yourself - what would happen if I didn't protect myself? Make a note of these assumptions.
- Plan an alternative - what could you do instead of protecting yourself? Decide exactly what those actions will be and when you will do them.
- After the event, reflect on what happened and whether your predictions were right.

(adapted from Butler, Grey and Hope, 2018)

APPROPRIATE IMPRESSION MANAGEMENT

In earlier chapters we discussed the importance of developing a professional identity based on your core values. These are the things that drive the person you are and reflect the image you have of yourself; this might include things such as honesty, openness and respecting others. For all of us it is important to try to align these things within our personal and professional lives but at times this can be challenging. When you completed the activity reflecting on any conflict between your front and back stage personas, you may have highlighted some personal values which seem to clash with aspects of the professional role. Some typical examples of this might be:

- You value open and direct communication but your colleagues prefer to show agreement with each other.

- You value truth and honesty; however, your manager is concerned about the impression given by the department's achievement data and wants you to be generous in your assessment of learners.

- You value working as a team but your colleagues want to showcase their own achievements.

- You value a solutions-focused approach and some of your colleagues are only able to see problems.

- You value autonomy but your organisation is keen on surveillance of activity.

As outlined in Kalvir's story, most people have a general desire to fit in with the people they work with and don't want to draw attention to any areas of difference. Similarly, people who do well in organisations tend to be those who fit the standard employee prototype, rather than those who challenge it. When there is a 'culture fit' encompassing shared values and personalities, individuals are likely to be more successful (Kristof-Brown, Zimmerman and Johnson, 2005). Even if we haven't read the research around this, most of us are inherently aware of it – as indicated by the phrase 'If your face fits.'

The challenge arises when aspects of culture do not sit comfortably with our professional identity. The education sector is, for the most part, dominated by formal hierarchies into which academic staff are expected to slot. Such structures are bound by formal processes but also by informal protocols in that there are certain approaches and ways of being that are likely to be valued more than others. This is where impression management is important as it sets the tone for social interaction. We all want to show the best versions of ourselves but also want to do so in a way that fits with our values and our professional identity. Impression management therefore needs to be appropriate and ethically sound. The following suggestions may be useful in helping you to find approaches that will be a good fit for you:

- Be consistent in your approach – review your values and remind yourself what is important. It is possible to disagree with others but still respect their views by taking a humanistic approach framed by unconditional positive regard (Rogers, 1961).

- Consider the use of appropriate self-disclosure. In order to bond with others it is important to share information about ourselves, but over-sharing can be problematic. Sometimes it is difficult to know where the line is between these two things so it is worth flipping the scenario to test whether or not to share something. This simply means that you think about your own response to somebody sharing that information with you. How would you feel if someone you don't know very well told you all the details of their latest breakup or divorce, or perhaps provided an account of all the mistakes they had made in the job? If the content makes you uncomfortable that is an indication that it might be a little too much information.

- Observe the local protocols – how do people interact in meetings or when they greet each other. This doesn't mean you have to follow suit but it does prepare you for what is considered acceptable within the context.

- Manage emotions – as outlined in Chapter 1, developing your EQ is likely to make you fit more easily into a new context. Emotionally intelligent people learn how to understand and manage their emotions; they acknowledge and accept feelings but are not slaves to emotional impulse.

- Have courage in your convictions – sometimes you need to make a stand. This may make you stand out from others but if your thoughts and ideas are supported by sound reasoning this will be seen as authentic.

- Respond appropriately to criticism. Burns suggests using the 'Disarming Technique' which is based on the law of opposites and the simple premise of finding some truth in criticism, even if it seems unfair. If we defend ourselves from criticism we may be proving that the criticism is justified; however, if we manage to find some truth in the criticism we immediately put the lie to rest and the critic no longer believes the initial criticism (Burns, 2020).

Much of impression management is based around the principles of effective communication and there is no single strategy that will create the 'right' impression. For that to happen we would need to know what 'right' is and of course that will vary from organisation to organisation. Communication underpinned by a strong professional identity and an authentic approach will simply present the image of someone who is self-aware and genuine – and that is a positive start to any impression.

CHAPTER SUMMARY

This chapter has considered the ways in which our role expectations influence our interactions. We have discussed the importance of authenticity based on professional values and where we might experience conflict within our roles. We have also explored the role of impression management and how to achieve this authentically by using our professional identity as a starting point. With those thoughts in mind we leave you with two questions to consider:

- How do you think your colleagues currently view you – are there any aspects of this impression that you would like to change?

- In what ways does your professional role match the principles of a fully functioning person – are there any aspects you could improve?

FURTHER READING

Brown, B. (2012) *Daring Greatly: How the Courage to Be Vulnerable Transforms the Way We Live, Love, Parent and Lead*, New York: Gotham.

Burns, D. (2020) *Feeling Great: The Revolutionary New Treatment for Depression and Anxiety*, Canada: PESI Publishing and Media.

9

COMMUNITIES OF DISCOVERY

In this chapter we will explore:

- How we construct learning with others
- The importance of teacher learning
- The influence of positive professional image

INTRODUCTION

In 1953 Airfix released a model of the World War 2 fighter plane, the Spitfire. For 2 bob (roughly 10p in new money), you could buy a 21 piece kit that allowed you to make your own scale version of the plane. It was an immediate success and the Airfix company flourished over the next three decades with a product range that consisted of an ever increasing array of planes, trains and automobiles, all recreated in miniature form and ready for the purchaser to link the pieces together to form their own version of the real thing. Of course, there was also another option and that was to buy the finished product. Plenty of Airfix's competitors offered completed models that required no effort from the buyer and could be put on display immediately. However, it was the Airfix version of a model, one where you had to work to achieve your goal, which flourished (David, 2007).

The idea of linking things together to create a whole is one that has firm foundations within the constructivist school of thought, an approach to learning that advocates the active construction of knowledge evolving from the experiences of the learner and stresses the importance of working together to co-create learning (Elliott *et al.*, 2000). This is considered to be a powerful way of embedding learning, and, as might be evidenced by the example at the beginning of the chapter, is probably far more satisfying for all concerned. Like constructing a toy model, it is the effort put in and the understanding of how things interact that motivates participants and leaves a lasting impression.

In this chapter we will explore the idea of communities of discovery – how these can form an approach to teaching and how they can provide opportunities for teacher learning.

CASE STUDY

Ully couldn't believe his luck when the job offer came through at the end of his PGCE course. He had been for an interview at the top-performing school in the area and almost immediately they had contacted him to offer him a job in their English department. He was delighted; the school had a reputation for excellent results and any pupils he had met always seemed to be polite and respectful. It seemed like a dream job.

A year later and Ully was feeling a little less enthusiastic about his new role. Whilst it was true that his learners were very well behaved, he sometimes wished they would challenge him a little more in class. They did seem very compliant and were very focused on assessment, which did tend to limit exploration of the subject. During his training Ully was consistently told that he must challenge learners and expect the same of them in order to construct learning together. Instead, what he was experiencing was groups of polite and focused sponges who soaked up his every word.

Ully understood the importance of passing exams, but the constant emphasis from the School Leadership Team on this aspect of the job made him think that his job was more akin to that of a drill sergeant, making sure that his charges were fully prepared for the examination at the end of the year. Although in some ways this was quite easy, it was also draining and he desperately wanted to try out more creative approaches.

Ully's experience is not an unusual one in UK education; the concept of schools and colleges becoming exam factories is well-established (Coffield and Williamson, 2011). When summative assessment is the overriding goal of the organisation, then this certainly has an impact on what teachers do. In this climate, it is inevitable that the teacher's job becomes instrumental in nature – helpful in achieving short-term goals such as exam success, but less so when trying to enhance curiosity, and as Ully was finding, this also meant that his own role lacked creative challenge.

HOW WE CONSTRUCT LEARNING WITH OTHERS

Constructivism sees knowledge not as a commodity, or something to be delivered, but as something which is constructed by individuals themselves (Thompson and Spenceley, 2020). This approach takes into consideration individual differences, all of the things that will have informed an individual's personal knowledge and world view. There are three key principles to consider:

- The first is that learners build new knowledge on the foundation of previous learning. So the role of the teacher is to help guide learners via the learning experiences.

- The second principle is that learning should be an active rather than a passive process. Meaning is constructed through engagement with ideas and concepts rather than being something that is received.

- Finally, learning is socially located and personal. This means that the role of the teacher changes from an instructor to that of facilitator.

By connecting new knowledge with existing learning, current mental maps are adjusted. Each person will do this in their own unique way as they are actively involved in the process of making sense of the new information. What is often difficult for teachers in this is the idea of letting go of control over classroom activities and therefore having less influence over outcomes. This is understandable, given the importance of learner achievement, but it is worth remembering that a constructivist approach is built on a partnership between student and teacher. Teachers still direct activities but use strategies which empower learners to take responsibility. This is done by using coaching and modelling approaches and putting in place scaffolds in the form of supporting activities.

Figure 9.1   Oh Captain, My Captain

REFLECTION

Think about the factors which usually influence how you plan your lessons:

- Are there standardised approaches within your setting?
- Are you expected to focus on specific outcomes?
- Is the lesson driven by learning objectives?
- Do you have complete autonomy in terms of what and how you teach?

Cultures within different settings inevitably influence how we carry out our day to day activities and those geared towards the co-creation of meaning will usually be open to approaches such as problem-based or discovery learning. Where the culture encourages greater uniformity and the role of the teacher is to lead rather than support, then introducing a constructivist-based approach can be more of a challenge, but the longer-term benefits are worth the effort: more engagement, the development of learner autonomy, enhanced retention and, perhaps most importantly, the generation of a culture which encourages curiosity and a love of learning. If you have ever watched *Dead Poet's Society* (essential viewing for all teachers), you will remember some of the approaches Robin Williams employed when trying to encourage his students to 'seize the day'. Active lessons which encouraged them to be individuals and take charge of their own learning. John Keating did employ a lot of methods which most certainly contravene today's health and safety guidelines, but the underlying principle still applies. Learning must be memorable.

SOCRATIC QUESTIONING

A constructivist approach – this method of questioning, named after Socrates, is specifically designed to allow students to explore gaps in their knowledge and also allow them to challenge their assumptions (Van Aswegen, Brink and Steyn, 2011). Whilst questioning is a staple of any classroom, many teachers use questions in limited ways, seeking confirmation that learning objectives have been met. The Socratic approach has a focus on encouraging critical thinking, challenging assumptions and widening perspectives. It is based on the use of six types of questions:

- *Conceptual clarification* – Can you give me an example of?
- *Probing assumptions* – What else could we assume?
- *Probing rationale* – What evidence is there to support this?
- *Questioning viewpoints* – What alternative ways are there of looking at this?
- *Probing implications* – How does this affect …?
- *Asking questions about the question* – Why did I ask you that question?

ACTIVITY

Look at the following dialogue and highlight the type of question that is being used.

Teacher: What would you say is the most effective leadership style?

Student: The affiliative approach is definitely the best.

Teacher: What do you mean by affiliative?

Student: It's a method whereby you allow followers to have a say in the decision making process.

Teacher: Good, but are there any other approaches that can be used?

Student: Yes, of course, democratic, autocratic, laissez-faire, but affiliative is the best option.

Teacher: Would everyone agree with you?

Student: Well no ... it wouldn't work in the army of course.

Teacher: So what does that mean in terms of leadership styles?

Student: Well, I suppose there are different points of view ...

Teacher: Exactly!

Constructivism isn't about using particular strategies, it is more about an overall approach based on the following principles:

• The development of new knowledge by the individual.

• Seeing learning as an individual process.

• Linking new learning with existing knowledge.

• Creating learning opportunities which involve interaction (Thompson and Spenceley, 2020).

Collectively these principles are designed to create a culture whereby students are able to explore concepts and construct their own knowledge with the support of the teacher. These are the first steps to developing a community of discovery.

THE IMPORTANCE OF TEACHER LEARNING

Learning can be transformative but for this to be the case we need to actively challenge current thinking. As we discussed in Chapter 2, our world view or 'map' is not the only way of looking at things. The way that we frame our understandings has a purpose in integrating information but it isn't based purely on accepted facts, it may also include supposition; as Dewey suggests, frames of reference: 'insinuate themselves into acceptance and become unconsciously a part of our mental furniture' (1910: 5). This means that they can also be limiting and we may need to seek out ways of extending our learning.

Lave and Wenger (1998) suggest this can be done through communities of social interaction and collaboration such as communities of practice (CoPs). These provide an opportunity for members to collaborate through the sharing of knowledge and resources and act as a forum for discussing ideas. The idea of CoPs became very popular in education circles around ten years ago and it is easy to see why the idea is attractive as, in principle, they provide a great platform for the co-construction of learning. However, for that to happen they do need to work in a practical way and this isn't always the case. There are four key reasons for this:

- There is often a low level one to one interaction – members take part in the events of the community but don't necessarily collaborate outside of this.

- Rigidity of practice – members already have their own ways of doing things and can be reluctant to integrate the ideas of others.

- Lack of identification – sometimes members don't identify with the group or see it as being meaningful for their work. Depending on how they are managed, CoPs can come across as a little esoteric by focusing on big picture ideas that aren't always easy to translate into the day to day.

- Practice intangibility – this happens when group members cannot visualise examples that they can apply to their own practice. In order for group members to see ideas as being useful they need examples of how they can be applied in concrete ways and for this to happen group members need opportunities to engage, share ideas and discuss how things have worked out in practice (Probst and Borzillo, 2008).

Most of us already belong to communities of practice – although they may not use that label. They are an integral part of professional life and may be formed within organisations or by external agencies, such as professional bodies whose aim is to promote collaboration in order to develop expertise within the field. Learning in this way is about social participation and when we become active participants, we have a forum for developing our understanding and enhancing what we do. However, that is unlikely to happen if participation is limited by any of the points mentioned above, so how we manage our interaction with CoPs is a very important aspect of their success.

MAKING COPS WORK FOR YOU

Participating in a CoP can be an exciting opportunity which provides a dedicated space for personal or professional development, but sometimes it can be difficult to know where to start. Communities exist within a range of disciplines and may take place within organisations or externally in the wider professional sphere; some are even international. There are a number of professional associations whose aim is to develop networks of practitioners in order to increase collaboration and the sharing of knowledge. These formal organisations also have an additional and important role and that is in elevating the status of the profession overall. This is perhaps even more important in teaching as it hasn't always had professional status.

How many groups did you have in your list? It is possible that this might include:

- Research or reading groups within the organisation

- Special interest groups such as those focused on pedagogy or assessment

- Member of a professional body, for example the Chartered College of Teaching or the Society for Education and Training.

Most networks are now supported by technology so it is quite easy to participate in training events or meetings. Online portals also offer access to large amounts of information in the form of blogs, discussion boards and publications. Some also have their own periodicals. However, as with many things, getting started isn't always a simple process. When you start investigating opportunities you will discover an array of opportunities but experience has taught us to be selective, firstly because of time limitations and secondly because not all opportunities are developmental. For this reason, it is worth spending time thinking about where your interests really lie and then considering what you want to get out of participating in a particular community. Once you start the search, lots of pathways will emerge and it can be a little overwhelming, so it is worth prioritising from the outset.

One consideration is whether or not membership is free – the costs can add up and subscriptions are normally annual payments rather than one-offs. CoPs can be very beneficial if you make them work for you, so here are a few things to consider:

- The purpose of the community – is there a particular focus? Some groups, such as professional bodies, have a very strong focus in terms of maintaining and enhancing practice; others, such as discussion groups, have more of a focus on idea generation.

- How the community operates – how and where do members meet? Is there a cost associated with joining? Many discussion groups are free and are based on small group interaction and informal communication, whereas most professional bodies have a formalised structure, charge a membership fee and tend to organise larger events such as annual conferences.

- Methods of participation – are there open discussion forums or more formalised channels of communication? Does the group have a journal or blog? Is this open access and can you share your own expertise using these vehicles?

The most important consideration is the benefits of participation and how this might inform your thinking and your practice.

MANAGING YOUR DEVELOPMENT

Getting involved in CoPs is only one way of taking charge of your development. There are also other things you can do to make sure you make the most out of the opportunities that present themselves. One obvious option is to consider studying; there are a variety of Masters programmes aimed at teachers and these can be very practically focused. In addition the Chartered College of Teaching offers the option of gaining Chartered Teacher Status (Chartered Status – chartered. college) and the Society for Education and Training have a similar route to achieving Advanced Teacher Status (Advanced Teacher Status – The Education and Training Foundation – et-foundation. co.uk). There is no shortage of formal opportunities for professional development, but for many people the most important thing (and often the most effective) is to take small steps aimed at specific improvements. If this is your favoured route then it is important to remember that it requires a supporting process, otherwise it ends up as an aspiration which is continually pushed to the bottom of the 'to do' pile. Two effective approaches for incremental and focused professional development are:

- Mentoring – finding someone with the relevant skills who can support and encourage your development. Or, if there isn't a mentoring programme in place, the first step might be to talk to others about setting one up.

- Setting goals and targets – use a formalised system of reflection linked to goal setting. This means committing regularly to open and honest reflection and choosing a process for structuring goals and targets. Two well-known approaches to this are SMART (the setting of targets that are specific, measurable, achievable, relevant and timebound) and WOOP. The latter is used less often so may require a little more explanation:

  o W – this is your *wish* and involves summarising what you want to achieve in 3–6 words, for example 'I want to run 5K'.

  o O – refers to the *outcome* and is about visualisation. What would it look and feel like to be able to run 5K? Visualisation provides the opportunity to embed a mental image of the achievement.

○ O – considers the *obstacle(s)* that might stop you from achieving your wish. This provides an opportunity to mentally prepare.

○ P – in this final stage you should *plan* what you could do to overcome any obstacles.

What is interesting about this approach is that it has a focus on making achievement real through the process of visualisation and at the same time puts in place contingency plans to overcome obstacles, making it more likely that we will achieve what we set out to do. This recognises that positive thinking alone does not actually prepare you for achievement and very often ends at the wish stage (Oettingen, 2014).

Figure 9.2   WOOPing goals

CREATiNG POSiTiVE HABiTS

In Chapter 6 we discussed how routine and habit can limit flexibility. That still holds true but habit can also be a force for good, particularly when we are trying to embed a new behaviour. As we all know, goals can sometimes be disheartening, particularly the long list of New Year's resolutions that we hope will change our life forever. How many times do you see people out jogging on January 1st, then limping along for a few days and finally going into hibernation for the rest of the year? The problem is not the goal itself but the way it is implemented. Many of us attack our goals like time is running out when perhaps we should be building them into our daily routines. According to Clear the secret to achieving your goals is to set up a support system (Clear, 2018). This approach switches the focus from achievement of the overall goal to the creation of a number of small, easy habits that can easily be integrated into life. This can be done in five simple steps:

1. Decide what your new habit will be – for example, 'I will spend 15 minutes reading education literature/writing a reflective journal every day'.

2. Create some simple rules to follow – it is important that these don't feel like an effort; for example, I will do this whilst enjoying my morning coffee.

3. Identify the cue – In this example the cue could be making a cup of coffee in the morning.

4. Establish a pre-habit ritual – this helps with the transition between activities and it is important that it is something enjoyable or at the very least something you don't mind doing; for example, before making coffee I will select a favourite mug.

5. Set up the environment – make the habit pleasant and easy to adopt. Have what you need to hand so that the process becomes seamless and eventually simply becomes a part of your day (Butler, Grey and Hope, 2018).

Teacher learning is so important for both teachers and learners, yet it is often not prioritised. The reasons for this may be institutional as well as personal and most of us would say we just don't have time. Whilst we can't create more hours in the day, it is possible to shuffle priorities a little and start to achieve the things we want to by making small, incremental changes and set up new habits in such a way that we can't fail.

ACTIVITY

Make a start

What do you want to achieve? Try to visualise this using the WOOP method. Then break down the goal into smaller steps and think about how you can accommodate these into your daily routines using the 5-step model. Even if you can only manage one step, over time this can make a significant difference.

THE iNFLUENCE OF PROFESSiONAL iMAGE

In Chapter 1 we introduced the idea of professional identity, which we described as an understanding of the professional role as well as the way you identify with the profession as a whole. We also suggested that a key part of this is to examine the values and ethics you might employ in your role. In Chapter 2 we discussed the importance of agency, the personal autonomy which informs action, and stated that agency is an essential component of identity and as such is something we need to construct for ourselves. Agency and identity are closely linked – they are pieces of the jigsaw which make up the picture as a whole and are really important aspects of being a teacher. Another piece of this jigsaw is professional image. This has always been a very tricky area for teachers as the role is subject to so much judgement, from so many people. Not surprisingly, 'Teacher bashing in the press' was listed by *The Guardian* as the second most popular reason for teachers leaving the profession (Marsh, 2015, online). Although this was published six years ago, there is plenty of anecdotal evidence to suggest that many teachers feel undervalued. One of the problems here is that everyone feels they have a say about education – and of course they do. This means that there is a very real likelihood that views will be based on different perspectives and as a result will be very mixed.

CASE STUDY

On a long train journey home, Alan was scanning the paper for something interesting to read and came across the headline:

Teachers are not keen on cutting short their Summer holidays to help students catch up

Muttering the words 'bloomin typical' under his breath he read on. The article discussed the impact of Covid-19 on children's learning and outlined the problem from a range of perspectives stating that those from privileged backgrounds, eager and able to learn, would be supported by parents and private tutors, whereas those from disadvantaged backgrounds would simply miss out. Alan nodded as this statement reinforced his views about 'the haves' and 'the have nots' in society.

The article went on to suggest that the teachers should forgo their holidays in order to support those learners who would not be supported at home. He was beginning to think that this reporter really knew their stuff, then he came across some quotes from people who had been interviewed:

Parents saying that this was just proof that teachers were lazy

Union reps saying that teachers were entitled to a holiday just like anyone else

School leaders saying that it wasn't feasible to put this plan into place

Teachers expressing concerns about effective pedagogy

By the end of the article Alan didn't know what to make of it and decided that the crossword might be a better option.

For most people education and teachers are inseparable, so if there is a judgement to be made about one it will almost certainly influence the other. Whilst we can't really do anything about how other people choose to judge us, what we can do is frame our professional image in positive ways which in turn will reflect positively on the profession as a whole.

CONSTRUCTING YOUR PROFESSIONAL IMAGE

You have probably heard the saying (usually accredited to author Andrew Grant) 'You never get a second chance to make a first impression', but how true is this? Sometimes we are told that it takes less than ten seconds for most people to form an opinion of you. Quite a scary thought isn't it? On first meeting, most people will take a sort of inventory of things like how you hold yourself, your mannerisms, smile etc. In addition, they are also making some decisions about character traits such as whether they think you will be trustworthy or not, and all of this based on rather scant evidence. What is even more concerning about this is that research suggests in fact it does not take someone ten seconds to make a judgement about you – it takes them less than a second! Using a series of experiments, Wills and Todorov (2006) looked into the time it takes people to make judgements about others and discovered that judgements were made after a very short period of time and were not changed when that time increased, suggesting that the first impression is very important. The good news is that, by managing your professional image, you have a good chance of making a positive first impression.

Writing about how to construct a professional image is something we want to add a 'handle with care' label to as the whole process is subjective. What one person sees as a confident display, another might view as hubris; add to that the general cultural sensitivities of a society that does not view self-promotion in the most positive light and we have an interesting cocktail. That said, there is no getting away from it – image is important and you will be judged on it. The information that follows is based on literature related to teachers' professional image, as well as anecdotal evidence and the information we have gleaned through our combined experience (which, if we toy with statistics, is around 60 years).

There are three key areas to consider here:

Relationships are a key aspect of the teacher's role so it is not surprising that this is something which should be managed. The key thing to remember is that relationships with learners, colleagues and managers must be appropriate. Whilst we don't necessarily hold with the 'don't smile until Easter' view of how teachers should be with their learners, we would also stress that however relaxed you are as a person, you do need to be conscious of boundaries. Learners often give the impression that they want their teachers to be friends, but what they really want is someone who displays the typical characteristics of a good teacher, i.e. someone who is supportive and understanding but is also able to create a positive and challenging learning environment. It is also important to remember the impact your interactions with colleagues will have on your professional image. This is often something we take for granted, but it is worth reflecting on how your colleagues might see you and whether or not this is the image you want to project.

Public profiles are something we cannot escape – they are everywhere. Most of us have interacted with one of more social media platforms and many people make use of social networking sites such as LinkedIn. Whilst many of these things are activities we do in our own time, we do need to remember that others will make use of them to get an impression, often before they meet you.

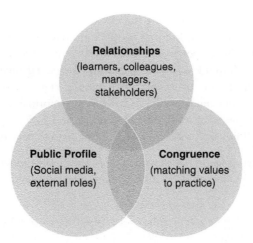

Figure 9.3   Aspects of image

The final consideration is that of congruence. This is something we have discussed in earlier chapters and is closely linked to authenticity. Things to think about are whether your online profile matches your written profile and the 'real' you. Sounds simple but when there are so many aspects to consider, it is easy to forget something.

Because image is such a personal thing we can't offer you a fool proof strategy for constructing your own; however, our top ten pointers would include:

1. *Choose the right associates* – this could be colleagues at work, external colleagues or being linked to CoPs that can enhance your development. That isn't about being exclusive but is *about* developing relationships that support your goals. It is also important to remember to make an effort to interact with everyone at work. Who you know is important but it is just as important to consider who knows you.

2. *Know your job* but admit you don't know everything. Owning up to your mistakes shows that you are genuine, but also remember not to blame yourself for everything as this can create an impression that you lack confidence.

3. *Keep your promises* – you don't want to get a reputation for being unreliable! To do this you need to focus on two key things: the first is not committing to things you don't have time to do and the second is about managing your time carefully.

4. *Develop emotional intelligence* – showing your emotions is absolutely fine and it could be argued is a healthy thing – but you also need to manage them. This can be a difficult area for a lot of people as they don't feel able to express emotions and don't want to be seen as 'emotional'.

5. *Be positive and respectful towards others* – this is an obvious statement and is really about keeping a check on yourself. We can all get drawn into complaining when things aren't going well and whilst you are not expected to be a robot, you do need to think about who you share your concerns with. An important consideration here is to openly praise others when you have an opportunity to do so.

6. *Keep your social media in check* – spending time managing your public profile is well worth the effort as this might be the only thing that people can link with you. A key consideration here is to keep your personal life personal. In a similar vein, think about what your email signature says about you. There is a trend to use this as a form of personal advertisement, for example by adding the latest publications or events you are planning. There are of course different views on the image this presents, but the key thing is to keep the information relevant – if you want to advertise your achievements all well and good, but avoid things such as daily affirmations or quotes – this simply dilutes the profile you are working hard to develop.

7. *Have the confidence to be yourself and stay true to your values* – genuineness is important and presenting an authentic image says something about your confidence. No-one is expected to be perfect – just real.

8. *Spend time building collegiate relationships* – be supportive to colleagues, share ideas, work together towards shared aims.

9. *Create a positive vibe* – we have said this in other parts of the book but it is worth mentioning again. This isn't necessarily about always being upbeat so much as it is about avoiding negativity.

10. *Look the part* – this is quite difficult for teachers as there isn't a particular look attached to the role. Indeed it is very flexible and in some settings quite casual. Looking the part is about checking in with what your personal presentation says about you.

There is no one perfect image for teachers, so some of these strategies will be more applicable than others. The best approach is to start by reflecting on the image you want to convey – then go back to the list and select some things to focus on.

CHAPTER SUMMARY

In this chapter we have considered the importance of co-constructing learning with a particular focus on how this can be employed for tutors' professional development. This has links to topics covered in previous chapters, in particular the need for teachers to develop their agency and form a strong professional identity. A further piece of the 'being a teacher' jigsaw has also been addressed: that of professional image. This can be quite a controversial topic and we have endeavoured to offer practical advice, which can be easily adapted in order to cultivate the positive professional image you want to project. Finally, we would like to leave you with the following questions:

- In what ways can you develop your professional learning?

- What strategies could you employ to enhance your professional image?

FURTHER READING

Coffield, F. and Williamson, B. (2011) *From Exam Factories to Communities of Discovery: The Democratic Route*, London: IoE Press.

10

IN TEACHING AND LEARNING EVERYTHING IS CONNECTED

In this chapter we will explore:

- The impact of systems on classroom practice
- How the environment influences our choices
- The teacher's role in developing teaching and learning

INTRODUCTION

In Chapter 6 we introduced the idea that we are all part of a system and we looked at the concept of feedback loops – the ways in which one action causes another reaction. This theory is based on developing an understanding of the interwoven nature of things and recognises the importance of taking into account the context within which activities take place. According to Bateson (1972), all things are connected and it is by discovering the pattern that connects them that we are able to develop a deeper understanding of how human activity is affected by its environment. In this chapter we will discuss how systems within organisations and at an individual level impact on teacher and learner development and on the wider education sector itself.

ORGANISATIONAL AND PERSONAL SYSTEMS

In Chapter 1 we indulged in a brief historical journey through some important milestones in the English education system. This provided a platform not only to discuss our own views on the overall purpose of education but also to consider how external factors, such as government policy, have influenced what happens in the classroom.

REFLECTiON

Think about how things work within your own setting:

- Do you have particular policy in relation to assessment?
- Is the collection of data important?
- Is there a focus on specific legislation?
- Do you have a particular lesson plan template that guides how you might structure your lessons?

The chances are there are a number of things that must be done in a particular way to be in line with the organisation's policies. Many of these things are derived from external guidelines or research. We don't always have full information about why we have to do certain things in certain ways but the requirement to do so is usually made quite clear. These policies, or formalised approaches, might include assessment procedures, guidelines for developing the curriculum or how we should provide pastoral support. They guide our practice and in turn, have an impact on the culture within the organisation and even on classroom practice.

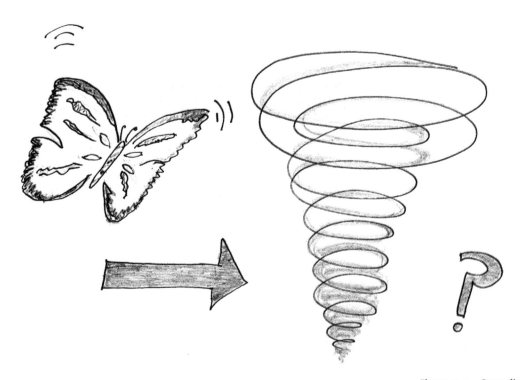

Figure 10.1   Butterfly

The 'butterfly effect' is built on the idea that small events can have a wide-ranging impact. The name was based on the work of meteorologist Edward Lorenz, who asked: 'Does the flap of a butterfly's wings in Brazil set off a Tornado in Texas?' – a question posed to illustrate the idea that complex systems can generate unpredictable behaviours and that even small variances can have a profound effect on outcomes. Lorenz was really observing the way that systems operate through interdependent cause-and-effect relationships that are often too complex to determine (Vernon, 2017).

It does seem quite extreme to think that something apparently unrelated can have a significant impact, but when you consider the systemic nature of life, patterns and connections are all around us, so the education sector can be seen as no exception. As outlined in Chapter 1, there are a number of apparently innocuous events that have actually had a significant impact on how we carry out our work. For example, Black and Wiliam's research 'Inside the Black Box' (Black and Wiliam, 2001) aimed at raising standards through assessment. This has had the intended impact of changing the structure of individual lessons in order to include more formative assessment, but it could also be argued that it has had a perhaps unintended impact on influencing the overall focus of teaching towards assessment and outcomes. In a similar way, Carol Dweck's (2017) research on mindset, intended to improve the way teachers help bridge the gap between where learners are and where they need to be, has helped to develop understanding of the importance of putting in place individualised support, but has the unintended consequence of creating an assumption that we can achieve anything if we develop a growth mindset. Small flaps of a butterfly's wings, creating classroom tornadoes.

FEEDBACK LOOPS iN ACTiON

In Chapter 6 we described feedback loops as a cause and effect model which takes into account different parts of a system, for example A influences B, and the response from B influences A and so on. Here is a simple example to illustrate the point:

A.   Barry prepares lots of detailed notes for his learners.

B.   The learners acknowledge the notes but most of the class leave them on the desk.

(B's influence on A) Barry questions the value of providing notes and makes the judgement that students don't read notes.

This represents a very simple cause and effect model which would probably continue with Barry's learners feeling neglected because he never provides them with notes and complaining about this when they are asked to evaluate his teaching! Simplistic cause and effect relationships are similar to the behaviourist model of learning, which is based on the premise that behaviour is a response to external events. However, feedback loops don't see this as a single behaviour–response link but recognise that behaviours provide feedback, which in turn alters responses. Just think of some of the incidents in a Jane Austen novel. In *Pride and Prejudice*, Elizabeth's relationship with Mr Darcy is peppered with misunderstandings, each forming part of a feedback loop which influences subsequent actions. She misinterprets his intentions and takes a haughty stance, he reads her haughtiness as disinterest and responds in kind. Round and round in circles they go, until finally the truth is leaked and all is well. This is a system in operation, actions are influencing reactions and reactions influence actions. Although this might seem obvious, it is surprising how often the second part of this loop is missed out in teaching and learning when systems are implemented and reinforced without taking in the full picture. Examples of this are particularly evident when considering approaches to managing challenging behaviour.

When we were undertaking our teacher training, behaviour management was seen as something to be applied, a set of strategies reinforced by yet another set of rules without any consideration given to the wider context. A lot of attention was given to how to manage others' behaviour, with very little attention being paid to why the behaviour was happening in the first place, or to the influence of the classroom culture. Fortunately, this is changing and the overall system is being taken into account. As Dix suggests: 'Outstanding management of behaviour and relationships is simply not skills led. Neither is it imported with "magic" behaviour systems ... in behaviour management, culture eats strategy for breakfast. Getting the culture right is pivotal' (2017: 2).

This is, at heart, a systemic approach and Dix cites many examples of where change has been implemented in this way. One is of a school that wanted to address all the pushing and shoving that was going on when pupils and staff were moving between classes. The school needed a solution. They could have followed standard protocol and built up a system of rules for everyone to follow; instead, they came up with the idea of 'fantastic walking' – a particular way of walking about the school. With complete consistency, pupils and staff adopt the same posture when walking about the school, hands behind their back, walking tall and proud. It was a cultural change implemented with positivity and had generated a sense of pride in the school. The school had thought about the whole context and what impact actions would have rather than simply applying a strategy to deal with a problem.

PERSONAL SYSTEMS

Systems don't just exist at an organisational level, they are also present at a personal level. Feedback loops provide information that results in repetition or avoidance of particular behaviours and if we are aware of them we can adapt our behaviours accordingly to achieve the outcomes we want – simple! The trouble is, it isn't simple, as many responses to events happen at a level beyond our conscious awareness, so what we think are choices probably aren't choices at all – we may simply be reacting to events in habitual ways and when we don't get the outcomes we want, we can make ourselves feel better by looking for forms of justification.

CASE STUDY

Karl was a very competent teacher currently working in an academy which was very driven by student outcomes. He liked his work, but he wasn't interested in moving up the promotion ladder ... he just wanted to teach and to find a position where his expertise was valued. Unfortunately, this was proving to be more difficult than he had imagined. In the past five years he had changed jobs three times and he couldn't understand why it was so hard to find something he liked. He always seemed to end up in the same situation - the work was fine, the team he worked with were OK ... but for some reason he had to endure ambitious male bosses that he didn't like and who didn't understand his lack of interest in promotion. After reflecting on his situation, Karl decided that this issue was caused by the men who had embraced the 'career teacher' persona and assumed everyone else wanted to do the same. Karl decided that the only way to find a job he liked would be to work with a female manager.

Karl was in a feedback loop. His story isn't particularly unusual in that he was feeling a little unsettled in his role and wanted to find some reasons for this. Work anxieties are often linked to our relationships with others and in this case Karl had detected the pattern that was problematic for him – his relationships with managers. He has also drawn some very definite conclusions about this. But what was missing from this reflection? Had Karl taken the time to reflect on the part he might be playing in this pattern? Is the problem purely down to Karl's bosses – different people in each of his jobs, or is there another pattern not yet uncovered? It may well be that the pattern repeating here is a little more complex than Karl originally thought – that's the thing with patterns, something may initially jump out at us and we pounce on it hoping it will resolve the issue, but there is the very real danger of addressing the wrong thing.

THE INFLUENCE OF ENVIRONMENT ON CHOICES

The five-part model (adapted from Padesky, 2020) illustrates the ways in which thoughts influence feelings, physical reactions and behaviours and shows that all of these happen within a given context. The model depicts how each of the four aspects interrelate and how a change in one can influence change in another. The model does take into account the influence of the environment and shows elements of how feedback from different parts of the system will influence responses – a nice illustration of the interwoven nature of experience. One thing that is less clear is how the impact of habitual behaviours, in both thought and action, will impact on our choices.

Sartre (2007) used the term *Transcendence* to describe the human capacity for openness and ability to define themselves. Because humans are capable of objectivity, they can put themselves into question and can distance sufficiently from the 'self' to question who they are and who they want to be. For Sartre, this idea represented freedom in that humans are free to choose how they interpret things, to decide what matters and what doesn't. We build our world through this freedom and at the same time create ourselves through our choices. Think about that for a moment.

REFLECTION

If you think about the major decisions in your life - like whether or not to go to university and what to study if you did? Job choices? How you chose your partner? The route you chose to follow once you had started your career? How many of these things were open, honest and balanced choices? How many of the decisions were influenced by circumstance and by things you may have experienced via feedback loops?

Figure 10.2 Five-point model

Generally, our choices are restricted by a number of things, such as our world view and the influence of others. In addition, they are made within a framework of habitual behaviour that influences our emotions and our thinking – at times it can be difficult to see if a choice was really a choice at all! Furthermore, we sometimes opt out of choices; decisions can be difficult and we are well aware that there will be consequences if we get it wrong. This in turn may lead to what Sartre calls 'bad faith', whereby we stick to what we see as safe, or familiar and in choosing to do so eliminate other options, so ultimately become victims of circumstance. We may tell ourselves we have the freedom to choose, but effectively we are choosing not to make a choice. This doesn't seem like a sensible option but think of the benefits … if things are deemed outside of our control, we may also deny responsibility and have the bonus of being able to apportion blame elsewhere. That does paint a picture of us being a somewhat helpless victim, but that isn't the case at all.

Figure 10.3   Bad faith

As teachers, we actually have a lot of influence, we just don't always realise it. There are a lot of strategies you can employ to help you take charge and make more informed choices. Some of these have already been discussed in previous chapters but here is a brief recap:

- Critically reflecting on your practice (Chapter 7)

- Claiming your professional agency (Chapter 2)

- Developing a strong professional identity (Chapter 1)

- Learning to communicate with honesty and compassion (Chapter 3)

- Managing your own behaviour (Chapter 4)

- Taking a flexible and informed approach to your teaching (Chapter 5)

- Raising awareness of the links between language, thought and action (Chapter 6)

- Adapting explanatory style and learning optimism (Chapter 6)

- Practising ethical impression management (Chapter 8)

- Learning through communities of discovery (Chapter 9).

All of these things are inherently connected in the professional role and together they make a whole. An important consideration is how we ensure that the 'whole' is representative of our values and closely linked to our professional identity.

THE TEACHER'S ROLE iN DEVELOPiNG TEACHiNG AND LEARNiNG

In our previous research we have encountered many stories of teachers who feel that their autonomy is consistently being eroded and at the same time they are experiencing greater levels of accountability (Thompson and Wolstencroft, 2018). This has had a significant impact on how teachers approach their roles, often leading to a preference for relying on tried and trusted methods rather than taking any risks and perhaps, more importantly, the generation of an understanding that they have no real agency (Thompson, 2018). This circumstance is even more evident for those who have management roles which, because of external pressures and a general lack of trust, appear to be framed as management by title rather than by authority – or, given the amount of direction that is provided, perhaps could be called management by numbers? (Thompson and Wolstencroft, 2021). The data is very real of course and is representative of how many teachers and managers feel – however, it isn't representative of how all teachers feel, and even more importantly, it doesn't mean that things have to be this way. When we start to think about it, we all have far more influence on our professional roles than we might think and because of this we also have the opportunity to develop teaching and learning despite any constraints from internal or external policy.

Everyone has a sphere of influence. This is normally made up of people within your network with whom your opinion matters. This could include close colleagues, people in similar roles in different organisations, friends, or people in any groups you might be a part of.

ACTiViTY

List all of the people you think are in your sphere of influence. Then list all the ways you think you might have influence with each of these people, for example: a colleague you work closely with who often seeks your advice about teaching strategies.

Your list probably included people in all the categories we mentioned earlier and maybe a few more. You might also have included your learners or perhaps any online networks you are involved with. The main point of this activity is to highlight the fact that you do have influence and as a result the ability to change the things that don't fit with your values. In short, whether we recognise it or not, we all have agency and as we suggested in Chapter 2, our view is that agency, even though it is situated in professional practice, is personal to individuals and provides the self-efficacy to prompt action. In addition, because of the influence of so many external and internal factors, agency is not something that will be handed out with your lanyard – it is something that must be claimed.

CHALLENGiNG ASSUMPTiONS

There are a number of assumptions made about teaching that, in our experience, have had a significant influence on how teachers enact their roles, for example:

- Ofsted knows best – the Office for Standards in Education was set up in 1992 and had a remit of raising standards in education. This in itself is a laudable aim, but is that what it has done?

According to Bassey (2010) and Coffield (2017), there is little evidence of this and the suggestion is that forms of external inspection may not be the best way to improve standards. Whilst an inspectorate has probably done some good in raising awareness of the importance of improvement, it is difficult to see how very diverse organisations can be judged fairly by one external body also driven by its own external requirements.

- Learning is evidenced by measurable outcomes – learning is not one-dimensional, it takes place in many forms and there are a wide variety of things which influence what has been learned and how that process takes place.

- Leaders know exactly what they are doing and should never be challenged – greater control measures within education have certainly placed leaders in positions of power, but does anyone know exactly what they are doing all of the time? Equally, the opposite assumption should be challenged – Leaders have no idea what they are doing and should always be challenged.

There are probably many more assumptions you could add to this list. As suggested in Chapter 7, reflecting on and challenging our assumptions is a significant step towards developing professional agency.

DEVELOPiNG YOUR MODEL OF TEACHiNG

Throughout the book we have considered the ways in which teachers can take charge of their professional roles by developing a strong sense of agency and a clear professional identity. A big part of this is thinking through your own model of teaching, one that is based on your values and beliefs about the purpose of education. In their review of 'great teaching', Coe et al. (2020) outline an interconnected model including four key elements:

- Having a good understanding of the subject and how it is learnt

- Creating a supportive environment for learning

- Managing the classroom to maximise learning opportunities

- Presenting activities and content in ways that activate students' thinking.

This is a useful starting point for developing your own approach. In addition, you might want to consider the ways in which you can continue to build your skills by:

- Taking ownership of your own learning and seeking out opportunities to build your knowledge and skills

- Seeking out communities of discovery through professional networks or research groups

- Finding an approach to reflection that can easily be built into your working week

- Building your sense of self-efficacy and claiming your agency

- Keeping your curiosity alive and being prepared to take creative risks.

When we are caught up in the day to day 'busyness' of teaching, it is easy to forget the connections between our own development and that of our learners, but if teachers stop learning, so too do their students. As we are influenced by our environment, so too are our learners influenced by us.

GROWING BUTTERFLIES

Earlier in the chapter we mentioned the notion of a butterfly effect – small actions which can have a powerful impact, sometimes in quite unexpected ways. Our previous examples outlined butterflies whose influence might be deemed less than positive (although that is entirely a matter of perspective), but of course we can also introduce butterflies which have a positive impact.

Figure 10.4   Magic butterflies

By making very small changes we all have the power to grow magic butterflies and encourage them to take flight in all of their splendour. As suggested by Quigley in his blog 'The Confident Teacher', 'Perhaps it is not sweeping changes from the top that make for *real, lasting change* at all. Perhaps one hundred per cent improvement is the result of one hundred small butterflies of change?' (Quigley, http://theconfidentteacher.com, accessed 6/2/21).

Small steps are important and there is much evidence to support this. In 2003, Dave Brailsford was appointed as performance director for the British cycling team who had been struggling in mediocrity for years (only one Olympic gold medal in 100 years, no Tour de France wins). Brailsford used a strategy referred to as 'the aggregation of marginal gains' (Clear, 2018: 13) and through this, set about making lots of small, incremental improvements to raise the team's game; small step after small step, each based on the idea of creating a 1% improvement. In the 2008 Olympic Games, the team won 60% of the cycling gold medals and four years after, set new Olympic and world records. A Brit even went on to win the Tour de France. Those tiny improvements turned out to be transformational.

By taking an incremental approach we can all make a difference. If we start by examining our values and focusing on the reasons why we became teachers in the first place, we have a sound foundation for building an education system that supports both learners and teachers. At times we will be challenged by the organisation we work in and by external bodies. We will also face hurdles presented by our students and colleagues – these things are all part of the systems which influence our practice. Perhaps the most influential is that presented by internal systems, by the way we think about, talk about and act on our experience. The good news is that this is also the system over which we have the most control. Developing new ways of thinking and being does present a challenge, but by taking small steps and making tiny improvements, we can all create some magic butterflies!

CHAPTER SUMMARY

In this chapter we have explored the notion that we are all parts of a system and have discussed the external and internal factors which influence professional practice. We have considered how our actions are shaped by our environment and how seemingly unrelated things may inform our teaching. This draws on all of the topics covered in previous chapters and highlights the importance of an integrated approach. By recognising the interwoven nature of things, we are equipped with a much broader and perhaps objective overview which helps us to make more informed decisions. We will all continue to face challenges in our practice but we are also all in a position where we can make small and positive changes. With that in mind think about the following questions:

- What would you most like to change about your teaching?

- What small steps can you put in place to help you make this change?

FURTHER READING

Bateson, G. (2000) *Steps to an Ecology of Mind*. Chicago, IL: University of Chicago Press.

REFERENCES

Adler, J. M. (2012) 'Living into the story: Agency and coherence in a longitudinal study of narrative identity development and mental health over the course of psychotherapy', *Journal of Personality and Social Psychology*, 102(2), 367–89.

Antonovsky, A. (1967) 'Social class life expectancy and overall mortality', *Milbank Memorial Fund Quarterly*, 45, 31–73.

Atkins, S. and Murphy, K., (1995) 'Reflective practice', *Nursing Standard*, 9(45), 31–37.

Bandler, R. and Grinder, R, (1975) *The Structure of Magic I: A Book about Language and Therapy*, Palo Alto, CA: Science and Behavior Books.

Bandura, A. (1977) *Social Learning Theory*, Englewood Cliffs, NJ: Prentice Hall.

Bandura, A. (1986) 'The explanatory and predictive scope of self-efficacy theory', *Journal of Clinical and Social Psychology*, 4(3), 359–73.

Bandura, A. (2008) 'An agentic perspective on positive psychology', in S. J. Lopez (ed.), *Positive Psychology: Expecting the Best in People*. Volume 1, New York: Praeger.

Barber, M. and Mourshed, M. (2007) *How the World's Best-Performing School Systems Come Out on Top*, London: McKinsey & Co.

Bassey, M. (2010) *'Time to Say "OFSTED Goodbye"*. Available at: Ofsted-goodbye (free-school-from-government-control.com) [accessed 6 February 2021].

Bateson, G. (1970) 'The message of reinforcement', in J. Akin, A. Goldberg, G. Myers and J. Stewart (eds), *Language Behavior: A Book of Readings in Communication* (pp. 64–72), The Hague: Mouton.

Bateson, G. (1972) *Steps to an Ecology of Mind*, London: University of Chicago Press.

Bateson, G. (2000) *Steps to an Ecology of Mind*, Chicago, IL: University of Chicago Press.

Batista, F. (2017) 'Is linguistic relativity a kind of relativism?', *Studia Semiotyczne*, 2, 201–26.

Becker, E. Goetz, T., Morger, V. and Ranellucci, J. (2014) 'The importance of teachers' emotions and instructional behavior for their students' emotions: An experience sampling analysis', *Teaching and Teacher Education*, 43(1), 15–26.

Bennett, T. (2013) *Teacher Proof: Why Research in Education Doesn't Always Mean What It Claims. And What You Can Do About It*, Oxon: Routledge.

Biesta, G. J. J. and Tedder, M. (2006) *'How Is Agency Possible? Towards an Ecological Understanding of Agency-as-Achievement* (Working Paper 5), Exeter: The Learning Lives Project.

Black, P. and Wiliam, D. (2001) 'Inside the Black Box, raising standards through classroom assessment', BERA Conference paper.

Bolton, G. (2014) *Reflective Practice: Writing and Professional Development* (4th edn), Los Angeles, CA: Sage.

Booker, C. (2005) *The Seven Basic Plots: Why We Tell Stories*, New York: Continuum.

Brookfield, S. (1990) *Becoming a Critically Reflective Teacher*, San Francisco, CA: Jossey-Bass.

Brookfield, S. (2012) *Teaching for Critical Thinking: Tools and Techniques to Help Students Question Their Assumptions*, San Francisco, CA: John Wiley & Sons.

Brookfield, S. (2017) *Becoming a Critically Reflective Teacher*, San Francisco, CA: John Wiley & Sons.

Brown, B. (2012) *Daring Greatly: How the Courage to Be Vulnerable Transforms the Way We Live, Love, Parent and Lead*, New York: Gotham.

Brown, B. (2015) *Rising Strong*. London: Vermilion.

Burns, D. D. (1990) *The Feeling Good Handbook*, Harmondsworth: Penguin.

Burns, D. D. (2020) *Feeling Great: The Revolutionary New Treatment for Depression and Anxiety*, Canada: PESI.

Butler, G., Grey, N. and Hope, T. (2018) *Managing Your Mind: The Mental Fitness Guide* (3rd edn), New York: Oxford University Press.

Canter, L. and Canter, M. (2001) *Assertive Discipline: Positive Behavior Management for Today's Classroom*, Santa Monica, CA: Canter & Associates.

Chandler, D. (1994) *The Transmission Model of Communication*. Available at http://visual-memory. co.uk/daniel/Documents/short/trans.html?LMCL=UucUH1 [accessed 9 February 2021].

Clear, J. (2018) *Atomic Habits: An Easy & Proven Way to Build Good Habits & Break Bad Ones*, London: Random House Business Books.

Cockburn, D. (2001) *Descartes: The Self and the World. In: An Introduction to the Philosophy of Mind*, London: Palgrave Macmillan.

Coe, R., Rauch, C., J., Kime, S., Singleton, D. (2020) *Great Teaching Toolkit, Evidence Review*. Available at: https://www.greatteaching.com/ [accessed 11 November 2020].

Coffield, F. (2017) *Will the Leopard Change Its Spots?: A New Model of Inspection for Ofsted*, London: Institute of Education Press.

Coffield, F. and Williamson, B. (2011) *From Exam Factories to Communities of Discovery*, London: Institute of Education Press.

Cornelius, L. and Herrenkohl, L. (2004) 'Power in the classroom: How the classroom environment shapes students' relationships with each other and with concepts', *Cognition and Instruction*, 22(4), 467–98.

Cothran, D., Hodges Kulinna, P. and Garrahy, D. (2009) 'Attributions for and consequences of student misbehavior', *Physical Education and Sport Pedagogy*, 14(2), 155–167.

Cowley, S. (2013) *The 7 Cs of Positive Behaviour Management*, London: CreateSpace Independent Publishing Platform.

David, M. (2007) *Airfix: Britain's Next Top Model?* Available at http://news.bbc.co.uk/1/hi/business/7131047.stm [accessed 30 January 2021].

De Houwer, J., Barnes-Holmes, D. and Moors, A. (2013) 'What is learning? On the nature and merits of a functional definition of learning', *Psychon Bull Rev.*, doi: 10.3758/s13423-013-0386-3. Available at: https://ppw.kuleuven.be/okp/_pdf/DeHouwer2013WILOT.pdf [accessed 8 June 2018].

Department for Education (2013) *Teachers' Standards Guidance for School Leaders, School Staff and Governing Bodies*, London: Crown.

Department for Education (2019) 'ITT Core Content Framework'. Available at: https://assets.publishing.service.gov.uk/government/uploads/system/uploads/attachment_data/file/919166/ITT_core_content_framework_.pdf [accessed 12 November 2020].

De Saint-Exupéry, A. (2000) *The Little Prince*, London: Macmillan.

Dewey, J. (1910) *How We Think*, Boston, MA: D C Heath & Co.

Dix, P. (2017) *When the Adults Change Everything Changes*, Carmarthen: Independent Thinking Press.

Duckworth, A. (2017) *Grit: Why Passion and Resilience Are the Secrets to Success*, London: Vermillion.

Dweck, C. (2006). *Mindset: The New Psychology of Success*, New York: Ballantine Books.

Dweck, C. (2017) *Mindset: Changing the Way You Think to Fulfil Your Potential*, London: Constable & Robinson.

Elliott, S. N., Kratochwill, T. R., Littlefield Cook, J. and Travers, J. (2000) *Educational Psychology: Effective Teaching, Effective Learning* (3rd edn), Boston, MA: McGraw-Hill College.

Ellis, A. (1991) 'The revised ABC's of rational-emotive therapy (RET)', *Journal of Rational-Emotive and Cognitive-Behavior Therapy*, 9(3), 139–72.

Esteläpelto, A., Hokka, P. K., Vahasantanen, K., Paloniemi, S. (2014) 'Identity and agency in professional learning', in S. Billet, C. Harteis and H. Gruber (eds), *International Handbook of Research in Professional and Practice-based Learning* (pp. 64–72), London: Springer.

Festinger, L. (1957) *A Theory of Cognitive Dissonance*, Stanford, CA: Stanford University Press.

Ford, E. E. (2004) Discipline for Home and School Fundamentals, Scottsdale, AZ: Brandt Publishing.

Foucault, Michel (1966/1970). *Les Mots et les choses: Une archéologie des sciences humaines*. [*The Order of Things*], Paris: Gallimard; New York: Pantheon/Random House.

Friere, P. (1970) *Pedagogy of the Oppressed*, New York: Continuum.

Gelb, M. J. and Miller Caldicott, S. (2009) *Innovate Like Edison: The Five-Step System for Breakthrough Business Success*, New York: Plume.

Gibbs, G. (1988) *Learning by Doing: A Guide to Teaching and Learning Methods*, Oxford: Further Education Unit.

Ginott, H. (1972) *Between Teacher and Child: A Book for Parents and Teachers*, New York: Macmillan.

Goffman, E. (1959) *The Presentation of Self in Everyday Life*, New York: Doubleday.

Goleman, D. (1996) *Emotional Intelligence: Why It Can Matter More than IQ*, London: Bloomsbury.

Gopnik, A. (2016) *The Carpenter and the Gardener: What the New Science of Child Development Tells Us about the Relationship Between Parents and Children*, London: Bodley Head.

Grant, A. M., Franklin, J., and Langford, P. (2002) 'The self-reflection and insight scale: A new measure of private self-consciousness', *Social Behavior and Personality: An International Journal*, 30(8), 821–36.

Harrington, R. & Loffredo, D. A. (2010) 'Insight, rumination, and self-reflection as predictors of well-being', *The Journal of Psychology*, 145(1), 39–57.

Hemingway, E. (1967) *Across the River and Into the Trees*, London: Arrow Books.

hooks, b. (2003) *Teaching Community: A Pedagogy of Hope*, New York: Routledge.

Illeris, K. (2007) *How We Learn: Learning and Non-learning in School and Beyond*, London and New York: Routledge.

Illeris, K.(ed.) (2009) *Contemporary Theories of Learning, Learning Theorists … in Their Own Words*. Oxford: Routledge.

Infed, *What Is Learning: A Definition and Discussion*. Available at: https://infed.org/mobi/learning-theory-models-product-and-process/ [accessed 24 October 2020].

Jeffers, S. (1988) *Feel the Fear and Do It Anyway*, New York: Ballantine Books.

Kolb, D. A. (1984) *Experiential Learning: Experience as the Source of Learning and Development*, Englewood Cliffs, NJ: Prentice Hall.

Korzybski, A. (1931) 'A non-Aristotelian system and its necessity for rigour in Mathematics and Physics.' Paper presented before the American Mathematical Society at the New Orleans, Louisiana meeting of the American Association for the Advancement of Science, 28 December 1931. Reprinted in *Science and Sanity* (1933), 747–61.

Korzybski, A. (1958) *Science and Sanity: An Introduction to Non-Aristotelian Systems and General Semantics*, New York: Institute of General Semantics.

Kristof-Brown, A. L., Zimmerman, R. D. and Johnson, E. C. (2005) 'Consequences of Individuals' fit at work: A meta-analysis of person–job, person–organization, person–group, and person–supervisor fit', *Personnel Psychology*, 58, 281–342.

Lave, J. and Wenger, E. (1991) *Situated Learning: Legitimate Peripheral Participation*, Cambridge: Cambridge University Press.

Lave, J. and Wenger, E. (1998). *Communities of Practice: Learning, Meaning, and Identity*. Cambridge: Cambridge University Press.

Marsh, S. (2015) 'Five top reasons people become teachers and why they quit'. *The Guardian*. Available at: https://www.theguardian.com/teacher-network/2015/jan/27/five-top-reasons-teachers-join-and-quit [accessed 3 May 2020].

Marzano, R. J. (1998). *A Theory-Based Meta-Analysis of Research on Instruction*, Aurora, CO: McREL. Available at: www.mcrel.org/PDF/Instruction/5982RR_InstructionMeta_Analysis.pdf [accessed 9 February 2021].

McLeod, S. A. (2018, February 05) 'Mind body debate', *Simply Psychology*. Available at: https://www.simplypsychology.org/mindbodydebate.html [accessed 9 February 2021].

Merrill, B. (ed.) (2009) *Learning to Change? The Role of Identity and Learning Careers in Adult Education*, Frankfurt: Peter Lang.

Merton, R. (1948) 'The self-fulfilling prophecy', *The Antioch Review*, 8(2), 193–210.

Mezirow, J. (1991) *Transformative Dimensions of Adult Learning*, San Francisco, CA: Jossey-Bass.

Mulford, P. (2011) *Thoughts Are Things*, Eastford: Martino.

Newberg, A. and Waldman, M. R. (2013) *Words Can Change Your Brain: 12 Conversation Strategies to Build Trust, Resolve Conflict, and Increase Intimacy*, New York: Plume.

Oettingen, G. (2014) *Rethinking Positive Thinking: Inside the New Science of Motivation*, New York: Penguin Publishing Group.

Owen, N. (2001) *The Magic of Metaphor, 77 Stories for Teachers, Trainers and Thinkers*, Carmarthen: Crown House Publishing.

Padesky, C. A. (2020) *The Clinician's Guide to CBT Using Mind over Mood* (2nd edn), New York: The Guilford Press.

Postman, N. and Weingartner, C. (1971) *Teaching as a Subversive Activity*, London: Penguin.

Probst, G. and Borzillo, S. (2008) 'Why communities of practice succeed and why they fail', *European Management Journal*, 26(5), 335–47.

Quigley, A. *'The Butterfly Effect in Schools'* (online). Available at: 'The Butterfly Effect' in Schools, the-confidentteacher.com [accessed 6 February 2021].

Robbins, A. (2001) *Unlimited Power: The New Science of Personal Achievement*, London: Simon & Schuster UK.

Robinson, K. (2010) *Changing Paradigms* (online) available at: https://www.thersa.org/video/animates/2010/10/rsa-animate---changing-paradigms [accessed 14 October 2020].

Robinson, K. (2017) *Out of Our Minds: The Power of Being Creative*, Chichester: Wiley & Sons Ltd.

Rogers, B. (2015) *Classroom Behaviour: A Practical Guide to Effective Teaching, Behaviour Management and Colleague Support*, London: SAGE.

Rogers, C. (1959) 'A theory of therapy, personality and interpersonal relationships as developed in the client-centered framework', in S. Koch (ed.), *Psychology: A Study of a Science. Vol. 3: Formulations of the Person and the Social Context*, New York: McGraw Hill.

Rogers, C. (1961) *On Becoming a Person: A Therapist's View of Psychotherapy*, New York: Houghton Mifflin.

Rogers, C. (1969) *Freedom to Learn: A View of What Education Might Become*, Columbus: Charles E. Merrill.

Rosenshine, B. (2010) 'Principles of instruction', *Educational Practices Series*, 21, 109–125.

Rosenthal, R. and Jacobson, L. (1968a) 'Teacher expectations for the disadvantaged', *Scientific American*, 218(4), 19–23.

Rosenthal, R. and Jacobson, L. (1968b) *Pygmalion in the Classroom: Teacher Expectation and Pupils' Intellectual Development*, New York: Holt, Rinehart & Winston.

Salovey, P. and Mayer, J. D. (1990) 'Emotional intelligence', *Imagination, Cognition, and Personality*, 9, 185–211.

Sartre, J-P. (2007) *Existentialism Is a Humanism*, New Haven, CT: Yale University Press.

Schön, D. A. (1983) *The Reflective Practitioner: How Professionals Think in Action*, New York: Basic Books.

Schramm, W. (1955) 'Information Theory and Mass Communication', *Journalism and Mass Communication Quarterly*, https://doi.org/10.1177/107769905503200201.

Seligman, M. (2006) *Learned Optimism: How to Change Your Mind and Your Life*, New York: Vintage Books.

Seligman, M. (2018) *Learned Optimism: How to Change Your Mind and Your Life*, London: Nicholas Brealey Publishing.

Stewart, I. and Joines, V. (2012) *TA Today: A New Introduction to Transactional Analysis* (2nd edn), Nottingham and Chapel Hill, NC: Lifespace Publishing.

Sweller, J. (1988) 'Cognitive load during problem solving: effects on learning', *Cognitive Science*, 12, 257–85.

Thompson, C. (2018) 'Finding the Glass Slipper: The Impact of Leadership on Innovation in FE', Fellowship project report, Further Education Trust for Leadership.

Thompson, C. (2019) *The Magic of Mentoring: Developing Others and Yourself*, Oxon: Routledge.

Thompson, C. and Spenceley, L. (2020) *Learning Theories for Everyday Teaching*, London: Learning Matters.

Thompson, C. and Wolstencroft, P. (2018) *No More Superheroes...Only Avatars?: Survival Role Play in English Post Compulsory Education* in Merrill, B., Galimberti, A., Nizinska, A. and Gonzales-Monteagudo, J. (eds.). *Continuity and Discontinuity in Learning Careers: Potentials for a Learning Space in a Changing World*. Leiden: Brill Academic Publishers.

Thompson, C. and Wolstencroft, P. ([2018] 2021) *The Trainee Teachers' Handbook: A Companion for Initial Teacher Training*, London: Learning Matters.

Thyer, B. A. and Pignotti, M. G. (2015) *Science and Pseudoscience in Social Work Practice*. New York: Springer, pp. 56–7, 165–7.

Van Aswegen, E. J., Brink, H. I. L. and Steyn, P. J. N. (2011) 'Application and evaluation of a combination of Socratic and learning through discussion techniques', *Curtionis*, 24(4), 68–77.

Vernon, J. L. (2017) 'Understanding the butterfly effect', *American Scientist*, 105(3), 130.

Willemyns, M., Gallois, C. and Callan, V. (2003) 'Trust me, I'm your boss: Trust and power in supervisor–supervisee communication', *The International Journal of Human Resource Management*, 14(1), 117–27.

Wills, J. and Todorov, A. (2006) 'First impressions: Making up your mind after a 100-MS exposure to a face', *Psychological Science*, 17(7), 592–8.

INDEX